Molding
Young
Athletes

To PSM Athletes
Helping every child
have fun in sports.

Darrell Erikson
Jun 3, 2004

Molding Young Athletes

How Parents and Coaches Can Positively Influence Kids in Sports

Darrell Erickson

Foreword by Jim Baugh, President, Wilson Sporting Goods Company

Purington Press
OREGON, WISCONSIN

Although the author and publisher have made every effort to ensure the accuracy and completeness of information contained in this book, we assume no responsibility for errors, inaccuracies, omissions, or any inconsistency herein. Any slights of people, places, or organizations are unintentional.

First printing 2004

ISBN 0-9743543-6-8
LCCN 2003111091

ATTENTION YOUTH SPORTS ORGANIZATIONS (LOCAL, REGIONAL, OR NATIONAL), SCHOOLS, CORPORATIONS, AND PROFESSIONAL SPORTS ORGANIZATIONS: Quantity discounts are available on bulk purchases of this book for educational purposes or fund-raising. Special customized books or book excerpts can also be created to fit your specific needs. For information, please contact Purington Press, POB 170, Oregon, WI 53575; call or fax 608-873-8723; www.puringtonpress.com.

TABLE OF CONTENTS

SECTION I: YESTERYEAR

SECTION II: YOUTH SPORTS TODAY

SECTION III: INSIDE

SECTION IV: YOU, THE COACH

SECTION V: THE SEASON

SECTION VI: THE FUTURE

Before It's Too Late

Slow your life down
Take time to play with your kids
Watch them grow and notice the little things
Treasure every moment and never wish for the future

They're growing up quicker than you know
Soon they'll be gone
You won't believe the rapid passing of time
Every parent feels this phenomenon

Denying time won't work
So enjoy them now
Enjoy every moment
Cherish today and every day

It will all be gone before you know it
So love, live, and play
Before it's too late.

FOREWORD

Throughout the ages, young boys and girls have engaged in various sporting activities. Games have always been a way for kids to pursue their number one passion—fun. True fun drives kids to enjoy life. Fun motivates them to spend many hours playing with other kids—competing, laughing, winning, losing, exercising, developing young social skills, and learning many of life's lessons. The term "fun and games" cannot be split. Fun and sporting games have always been the key to much youth happiness.

Today, we see millions of young people in all types of sports. As the president of Wilson Sporting Goods Company, I see a great opportunity to help our kids. There are so many fantastic lessons they can learn and carry into adulthood. And what a joy they provide to their family members and friends who participate as loyal fans. More kids than ever are engaging in organized sports. But in life and in sports, even with all the great opportunities our kids have, negative influences can creep into the picture.

Unfortunately, many parents and coaches damage the youth sports experience. We all know people who are positively motivated but cannot use their good intentions in productive ways. Youth sporting games should be good for kids, but sadly, in many cases we have organized the fun out of organized sports. Something is missing from the equation. Every parent and coach needs a solid resource they can use season after season. It is our job as adults to help each young person grow as they participate in their chosen sporting activity. We should use every tool at our disposal to mold their minds and bodies during the short time the good Lord loans them to us. We must discard our selfish motivations and eliminate our negative personality traits that become obstacles to the kids' overall enjoyment of *their* games. Many adults have lost true perspective and forgotten the games are for the kids. Parents and coaches desperately need an excellent resource tool that will teach them how to positively help their kids. There is a void of common-sense instruction in today's complex world of youth sports. This book fills the void. It is the missing tool.

Am I saying parents and coaches don't have any role in youth sports? Not at all! We have a critical role. Today's organized structure of athletic programs demands our presence and involvement. But our primary responsibility as an adult requires a proper vision. We have it in our power to make youth sports a great experience for everyone. We cannot forget that our true focus must lie with the kids, in the kids, and for the kids. Too many parents today seem to think it's all about adult games that adults are asking their kids to play. Kids want to play *their* sport and have fun in *their* sport in *their* own creative way.

My job is to provide you and your young athletes with the best sporting equipment in the world so that each young person can perform to his or her maximum potential. Your job as a parent or coach is to develop the mind and body of every young athlete to help them attain their number one goal—fun. With fun, good things happen. They learn, grow, stay involved, and make lifelong commitments to positive physical activity.

Together, we can meet these awesome challenges. The book in your hands will help you do your part. There are many books on the market that attempt to help adults as they work with kids. I've read a lot of them, but they focus on the physical and technical aspects of a single sport. Some may devote a few limited chapters to helping young people from the inside out, but none are as excellent as this book. They all miss the bull's-eye. The following pages will take you on a wonderful journey into the world of youth sports. As a parent or coach, novice or veteran, you will gain tremendous insights so that you can positively influence all young athletes. You will be instrumental in helping kids develop critical traits such as: positive internal motivation, positive mental control, an attitude as a winner in life, the ability to persevere, how to be a good winner and loser, and how to perform at their physical and mental peak. And through it all, you'll help them have fun. You will also develop a sense of your own involvement and responsibility as an adult interacting with young people. There is not a better book on the market. You all dedicate a lot of time and money on athletic gear, fees, travel, uniforms, and other sports costs. The small investment you make in this book will reap tremendous lifelong dividends for you and for your kids.

Please enjoy and implement the things you are about to discover. Thank you.

— *Jim Baugh*, President
Wilson Sporting Goods Company

PREFACE

Who-What-When-Where-Why?

For many years, in many different sports, with many teams, I've often asked during "bad" performances, "Why can't someone write a book for all coaches and parents that helps the team have fun and perform to its optimum potential on any given day?" There was never a good answer.

In 1999, several other scoutmasters from our Boy Scout Troop and I took 15 boys to Philmont, a high-mountain adventure camp in New Mexico. On the train while returning home, I was reflecting on the magnificent experience and contemplating the meaning of life. It was on that train that I was inspired to write the book all coaches and parents of young athletes so desperately need.

From that day to this, the journey has been filled with many ups and downs. I have learned much. Had I been able to read a book like this while I was a new coach, I would have avoided a lot of mistakes. Now my mistakes (opportunities to improve) and my successes can benefit you. My hope is that you can enjoy and use this book as you interact with your own kids and help them enjoy their sporting activities.

—*Darrell Erickson*

ACKNOWLEDGMENTS

I give special thanks to my incredible wife and our three children. My wife Patti has always been the rock in our family, keeping me grounded in the things that make life so wonderful. And she was a great listener during our daily three-mile walks as I developed this book. Our kids, Heather, Steven, and Craig, have welcomed me as their coach, their dad, and their playing partner. Without my family, this book would not exist.

Appreciation goes out to:

Todd Kane—he gave me my first coaching position with our sons.

Bob Millar—his visionary insights into young people and organized sports acted as a sounding board for my own ideas and philosophies. Bob is a true friend.

Pam Haese—I thank her for her "soccer mom" wisdom and suggestions on how to improve this book.

Cathy Smith—she's been my computer wizard. Whenever I had to learn a new skill or fix a self-inflicted error, she always helped me.

Jim Baugh—as president of Wilson Sporting Goods Company, he has a passion for kids and our youth programs. He tirelessly supports the PE4LIFE initiative (PE4LIFE.com) in this country that was established to promote strong public school physical education programs. His Foreword is very positive and powerful.

Jim Hutslar, Ph.D.—as the founder and CEO of the North American Youth Sport Institute (www.naysi.com), he provides many excellent tools for coaches, parents, and all interested adults who interact with our young athletes.

I want to thank my agent and publicist, Henry Holmes, for his hard work and commitment to helping young athletes. Gratitude also goes out to Jerry Stroud for his support and guidance. Both men are leaders in their fields and have become my friends. I thank the many men and women who have acted as my assistant coaches. They tolerated some unconventional ideas but I hope now they can see the benefits of my coaching techniques. Special gratitude is extended to About Books, Inc., for their excellent help in the pre-production process. And I give tremendous thanks to umpires, referees, and judges who invest their time and efforts for the overall good of youth sports. They deserve our admiration and gratitude.

I thank my mother for my family values. And God, for everything you've given, thank you.

INTRODUCTION

We've all heard it. We've all said it. "Eighty percent of the game is mental, twenty percent is physical." Yet we as coaches and parents dedicate most of our instruction time to the physical aspects of the game. Why? All across the country kids attend sports-related camps and clinics that emphasize the physical mechanics of various sporting activities. There are many books and tapes devoted to physical advancement. But this knowledge is only beneficial if players are motivated to internalize the skills they learn into optimum levels of performance.

How do we help them accomplish this? There are few limited resources available on the mental side of the game, the mental side of the team or the mental side of the individual player. Most of these psychological books are from doctors, child psychologists, and sports psychiatrists. Those people know a lot but have a difficult time transferring their vast knowledge and education into a usable tool the average parent or coach can use to effectively mold young athletes. I have taken their key ideas and simplified them. Many of their direct quotes have been interspersed into this common-sense, easy-to-use, and easy-to-implement book. This book will focus on your role as a coach or parent of young athletes in the mental development of individual players and the team. It will help you understand how our youth sporting programs have changed and will aid you to effectively work within the sporting environments of today and tomorrow.

There are coaches of young athletes and there are parents of young athletes. Both have significant roles. As coaches, our goal is obviously to turn a group of individuals into a team—a team that

1

controls its own destiny, a team that comes to the field or court or rink to play its best. As parents, we want our children to develop physically and mentally through positive involvement in sporting programs. Before we can help our young athletic teams or individuals, we must understand the dynamic mental framework of young males and females. This book will help coaches influence all players and determine which team shows up: the team that is motivated, self-driven, and possesses an intensity to play its best. At the same time, it will also help parents to positively influence and inspire individual players.

As you read the pages and chapters that follow, various comments and ideas will trigger thoughts to inspire you as a coach. For parents, there are many philosophies and concepts that will assist your efforts to positively guide your own child. Parents ultimately support and supplement the coach's efforts. Please consider this book a practical reference. Highlight specific sections and mark the margins for review season after season.

Note to coaches: You are in the trenches. It's not easy. You are the people talking the talk and walking the walk. Not only will *Molding Young Athletes* assist you season after season for your particular sport, it will help parents understand what you're trying to accomplish. It will draw them into your world of coaching. Recommend *Molding Young Athletes* to all your parents and you'll be amazed at how knowledgeable and empathetic they will become toward you and your responsibilities. As they practice the philosophies prescribed in the following chapters, they will become your army of informal assistant coaches, helping you guide today's youth and tomorrow's adults.

Note to parents: A major focus of this book is dedicated to coaches of youth teams and will provide them with tremendous insight regarding the development of their team and the individual players. You will discover much about the role of coaches. You will also learn a lot about your own role as a parent of a young athlete. As you read the following pages, many of the topics directed at formal coaches will mirror your personal interaction with your child. Every parent who reads this book will gain strong insight into the mind of a player and learn how to positively influence a young athlete. Your child and the team will have a much better experience if their coaches purchase, read, and implement this book.

Author's note: You will note periodic references to "we coaches" on various coaching topics. These discussions are directed to the complicated world of coaches. Yet most of the information presented in *Molding Young Athletes* will pertain to coaches and parents alike, and offers valuable perspectives for all readers. As you proceed through the following chapters, you will wear the hat of a coach, a parent, and a player.

Thank you for your dedication to our youth and our future.

SECTION I

Yesteryear

Notes and Thoughts

CHAPTER 1

The Good Old Days

Games sure were different back then

In the beginning there were the heavens and the earth. And on the flat spots of the earth young people gathered to run and kick and throw. Thus began youth sports.

Once upon a time, when we coaches and parents were just kids, time seemed endless. Each new day ran into the next and the next. Sports seasons had no beginning or end and we played whatever game appealed to us at the moment. Weather or Mom's suppertime usually determined a game's length. Long ago it seemed like there was much more spare time than kids have today. All in all, boys and girls enjoyed a less structured lifestyle with more time on their hands.

Simple Life

Our society has changed. Years ago there were more kids living in the open spaces of our country than today. More kids lived in agricultural areas and kids in the cities had more available space. There were only three main television channels: NBC, ABC, and CBS. Television was not the strong influence it is today, and there were few shows broadcast that held a kid's attention (except cartoons).

Distractions and Obligations

In past years there were fewer distractions than the large number that face today's kids. The kids of yesterday were not bombarded with an information society filled with activities and leisure time options. There were fewer demands within a child's less complicated sphere of life. Homework was not what it is today and kids focused primarily on the three R's: reading, writing, and arithmetic. Today's kids have many more school-related activities than kids in past years. Long ago kids had more opportunities for spare time activities like sports.

Family life was different. There were more traditional families with two parents running the show. In general, dads focused heavily on their work and more moms stayed at home during the day. There was less mom/dad pressure on kids to participate in formal sports than the pressures put on today's young people.

In yesterday's society, there was a greater acceptance of responsibility in the area of doing work at home. Chores were part of a kid's life and were done more willingly than by kids today. Also in today's richer society, kids perform fewer home chores because more money is available in the home to simply hand to a young person. Overall, kids of yesteryear experienced less of the pressures seen by kids today. Their lives were not as strictly organized, and they were not subject to the time-crunch lifestyles of today's youth.

School Sports

The entire realm of school sports was limited in past years. There were fewer sporting opportunities for kids to participate in. Kids became exposed to school sports in one of two ways: first, physical education (phys ed), which has always been a grassroots introduction for millions of kids to various competitive activities, and second, through organized after-school spectator sports. The primary spectator sports (and many times the only ones available) were football and basketball. Minor sports possibly included swimming, track, baseball, wrestling, and tennis if there was enough money, interest, and coaching. With limited sports available, there were fewer students signing up and playing. In his book, *Sport in Society,* author Jay Coakley summarizes:

> The vast majority of these sport programs were for boys between the ages of 8 and 14. They emphasized competition as a means of building the achievement orientations that would hopefully lead to personal success and community growth. Until the 1970s, girls' interests in sports were largely ignored in most countries. Girls were relegated to the bleachers during their brothers' games and given the hope of growing up to be high school cheerleaders. Then the women's movement, the fitness movement, and government legislation prohibiting sex discrimination (Title IX in the United States) all came together to provide an impetus for the development of new programs. During the 1970s and early 1980s these programs grew to the point that girls in North America have almost as many opportunities as boys. (Coakley, p. 105)

Although important, school spectator sports were not the dominant activity of the day. Of course they existed, but they were highly organized and had limited participation from the overall student body. So for kids to enjoy any sporting activity, they usually had to organize their own games with their neighborhood friends. In the next chapter, let's look at just how kids back then got together and played.

Chapter Highlights
to Improve Your Game Plan

▲ Kids of yesteryear had simpler lives than kids of today and there were more traditional family units.

▲ Kids had fewer organized sporting opportunities than they have in today's youth sports world.

CHAPTER 2

Backyard Diamonds, Courts, and Fields

Creative playing conditions

Did you ever slide into a second base made of a crumpled shirt or old piece of wood? Ever play football with no out-of-bounds lines? Ever play tennis in the street without a net? Ever play basketball on gravel with a hoop nailed to the side of the garage or barn? Did you ever conduct your own track-and-field race events by running to a far-away tree, touching it, and returning to the starting point?

When we were kids, we used our creativity to play various games. Many of us had no formal facilities so we had to use our vivid imaginations to set up playing conditions acceptable to our "not so high" standards. In those days, we created our own game facilities and were proud of our creations. We played and had fun under unstructured and sometimes adverse circumstances. Our time-frame perspectives ran from sunup to sundown and even later if we felt like it. We played football and baseball beyond the times today's "organizers" would allow. We played in the dark on many evenings and it was no big deal because we adjusted and were having fun.

Baseball/Softball

This sport offered great opportunities for kids to use their imaginations. In the country, kids used someone's backyard for a makeshift diamond. Trees and shrubs were the bases. Imaginary visual lines between home plate (a hole in the ground or someone's glove) and some faraway objects were the out-of-bounds lines. Closer to the city many kids played in vacant lots. Again, imagination was the key. Bats were made of anything long and skinny. Stickball was popular. Games were held in streets with light traffic and various items or spots were used as bases.

Basketball

Kids of yesteryear usually played basketball with one hoop and a dilapidated backboard. They congregated at someone's driveway (often gravel) and split into teams. Rarely was there a nice clean net. Someone would draw a line for free throw, but it was hardly used. Did you ever notice there were fewer fouls when kids played on their own? Again, the boundaries were rough lines somewhat resembling a half-court.

Soccer

Until recently, this was not a well-known sport. Kids had no idea of the formal rules of play and soccer was not a popular pastime. Just like the other sports, the boundaries and sidelines were fences, sidewalks, roadway boundaries, or other imaginary lines.

Football

This has always been a popular kid's sport. Everybody gets to play and positions are easily rotated to be "fair." Kids made their own fields with sidelines and end zones as best they could. If first downs were an option, they would leave a shoe or some other marker by the original spot and pace off 10 yards as the offensive team progressed. Usually though, the team with the ball only had four downs to score. This kept the game moving rapidly and made it more fun.

Hockey

In America's northern climates, outdoor hockey was always an option in the winters. Frozen ponds or ice rinks could be used. Goals were easily marked with a pair of someone's boots. Sticks were sometimes the real things but often they were just that, sticks. Pucks could be anything small and controllable, even a soda can.

Tennis

Tennis has been a sport restricted to the availability of courts and as a result did not enjoy the popularity of other individual or team sports. It had the image and reputation of a "rich person's" sport. Any pickup tennis game by kids was usually short-lived and full matches were rare. As a recreational activity, tennis did not have the mass appeal for kids searching for fun.

In addition to the above activities, there was kickball, four square, 500, dodgeball, simple tag, hide-and-seek, capture the flag, red rover, Simon says, jump rope, and many others. All these games were ruled by the kids and their imaginations.

Equipment

We've all seen gear used by kids in earlier years. Much of the equipment was old and secondhand. Old baseball gloves, worn-out footballs, old basketballs, and hand-me-down equipment were all kids could get. There was no real protective gear for catchers or goalies or football players. Kids wore normal street tennis shoes (if they wore shoes at all). There was not a lot of money spent on the latest fashionable gear and clothing.

So What?

So what did all this unstructured activity on informal facilities with less than optimum gear do for the kids of yesteryear? They developed the ability to govern themselves. If there were disputed calls that could not be resolved quickly, the famous "do over" was enacted. Kids made calls on close plays in an atmosphere of trust. Cheating was not considered acceptable among friends. Kids developed a sense of fair play and a feeling of good sportsmanship toward the other players. In the minds of the kids, all these recreational activities were for the purpose of having fun and passing time. The kids were not out there primarily to work on a specific skill or for some other artificial reason. Their focus was purely for the enjoyment of the game. In the next chapter, we'll review the factors that motivated kids to engage in various sporting endeavors.

Chapter Highlights
to Improve Your Game Plan

▲ Kids used their creativity to design and play their games.

▲ Favorite sports were baseball, basketball, soccer, football and hockey.

▲ Equipment and facilities were very sub-standard compared to today, but that didn't matter to the kids.

CHAPTER 3

Motivation

Why did kids play games?

In past years, what made kids get off the couch and go play ball? Why did kids gather to participate in a physical sporting activity? How did groups of boys and girls prepare to enjoy a game of their choice? The answers can be found within the realm of motivation and desire. Motivation is a powerful internal factor when we look at youth sports of yesterday and today. This chapter deals with the variety of things that motivated kids of yesteryear. You'll recognize many of the same traits that continue to motivate kids of today. Jay Coakley explains to us:

> When children get together and play on their own, they are interested in four things:
> 1. Action, especially action leading to scoring
> 2. Personal involvement in the action
> 3. A close score (that is, a challenging or exciting contest)
> 4. Opportunities to reaffirm friendships during the game (Coakley, p. 106)

Kids love action and being involved in the game. They love lots of scoring activity that results from much action. High scores and close scores make the game more exciting and more fun for all participants.

Fun

First and foremost, kids have always been and still are motivated by fun. Let's look at this simple but complicated term "fun." In yesteryear, fun involved kids doing what they wanted to do and enjoying it. It usually meant being with friends and having a positive experience. In Chapter 8, the deeper psychology of fun and its evolution will be discussed. For the purposes of kids long ago, fun was simple and each kid was drawn to it like a moth to a flame. They might not have been able to define it but they knew it when they experienced it. Having fun has always been a true internal motivator of young people to engage in any sporting activity.

Friends

Another motivating focus of most sports participation is being with friends. Sports activities provide kids the opportunity to make new friends and be with others they enjoy spending time with. Sports are "people-focused" activities and promote involvement with others. Being engaged in youth sports has always meant being part of the group.

Imagination

In past years sporting games have given kids a tremendous chance to utilize their imaginations. Kids constantly improvised various game situations and rules. Kids decided when a particular game would end. They determined all aspects of the game being played. This format led to kids taking ownership of their own game conduct and their level of enjoyment. It was their game.

Limited Self-Improvement

A small motivator in kids was the opportunity to show some improvement in their own levels of skill. Sporting games have always provided a chance for kids to challenge themselves to improve. Kids would turn a skill drill into a fun game, even if they were alone. Many kids would throw a ball against a wall or shoot baskets alone or some other form of inner competition. They would give themselves a target, such as 10 free throws in a row, 10 catches in a row, or some other goal. They'd turn routine repetition into a game of fun. As a result, kids improved their skills year after year. Even today we can see kids engaging in individual repetitive "games" of fun and improving at the same time. It helps their egos and gives them the chance to compete with the neighborhood superstars.

But for the most part, self-improvement was a by-product and not the major focus. The entire primary motivation was a personal internalized focus on fun and friends. Scores were kept and kids enjoyed the games more if there was a lot of scoring. It was more exciting for the players if the game was relatively close. For example, an early big lead by one team or person can diminish motivation by both sides and eliminates much of the fun. Kids have always thrived on fun. The next section brings us to the present status of youth sports today and illustrates how many things have changed.

Chapter Highlights
to Improve Your Game Plan

▲ The main motivation for kids to create and play their own games has always been for fun.

▲ Other childhood motivations to participate in fun and games were being with friends, using their imaginations, and self-improvement.

Youth Sports Today

Notes and Thoughts

CHAPTER 4

Structure Versus Pickup Games

How things have changed

Do you ever travel around and notice empty fields and courts? Do you ever wonder why no groups of fun-loving kids congregate like we used to do? Ever find yourself lamenting how kids today should be out there playing, having some fun, and learning the game of (you fill in the blank)? There is a difference today in the way young kids view pickup games. Let's look at some recent trends that have both helped and hurt various aspects of youth sports.

Trends

There was a time when kids would contact a bunch of friends. They would decide what sport to play and where and when to meet. This simple format was the way most games (outside of school sports) began. Throughout the game, other friends would join in or leave depending on circumstances. This "free substitution" made team adjustments easy. The players always tried to keep the teams somewhat balanced and "fair" based on perceived levels of skill.

This was informal yet quite effective. Obviously these types of pickup games still occur today, but they are less frequent than in past years.

Organized Activities

When we compare the huge scope of informal unstructured games of yesteryear to today, we see a different complexion to how kids and grownups approach sports. There are many organizations and groups involved locally and nationally. Just a few examples include: national youth sports organizations, national service organizations, national religious organizations, regional youth organizations, state school activity associations, local school districts, local service clubs, municipal recreation departments, and private sports clubs.

Today we have rigidly timed practices with definite beginnings and endings. Often there are other practices or games preceding or following our allotted court/field/diamond times. Also today, our games are on set schedules and time limitations. High school sports have always operated under the strictly organized formats being detailed here, but now we see this same structure for practices and games for many more young kids and their activities. Sporting options for today's young athletes have been greatly expanded from high school levels to the younger levels of middle/junior high and even grade schools.

However, we are seeing an alarming trend. Much to the detriment of many kids, schools all across the United States are dropping phys ed instruction, depriving kids of the exposure to basic sports they used to get. Solid physical healthy lifestyles are not being introduced to millions of kids and we all see the results in overweight and inactivity. Unfortunately for many young people, the entire landscape has changed.

Today's youth sports are conducted on formal fields, courts, and diamonds. There are relatively few improvised fields like we discussed in earlier chapters. The facilities used in today's sporting world are well maintained, manicured, and state-of-the-art. Most kids playing or practicing under these conditions have never had a tree for first base or a driveway for the end zone, (this would be a perfect time to say kids of today don't realize how lucky they are, but we won't).

Many Adults

Another phenomenon witnessed in recent years has been the huge influx of adults getting involved in youth sports. This can have benefits for all involved, but it certainly changes the face of sporting. We see:

▲ Coaches

▲ Team managers

▲ Assistant coaches

▲ Athletic organizations

▲ Support committees

▲ Interested individuals

▲ Parents

Throughout this book, we'll look at many of these different adult levels of involvement and their impact.

Organization Outcomes

Transport your mind to earlier days when you were a kid. Imagine a fall day when you and a few friends would rake up a big pile of leaves. Your only objective was to run and jump and get buried. Think of the fun and pure joy you experienced from that kind of play. You would be giddy with delight. Nothing else in the entire world mattered. You were playing and having fun. And you managed to do it all without any adult guidance or coaching. With the dominance of structure in youth sports, kids have lost the freedom they enjoyed years ago when most youth sports (except limited school activities) were controlled by the kids. Kids playing informal games made their own decisions and focused on action. In today's controlled format with time and game limitations, kids feel like pawns on a chessboard or puppets on a string. In structured games and practices, the focus is on rules and adults. Young people prefer an atmosphere of recreational games played for fun but practices and structured sports have replaced games. Practices are now equated with monotony, drill, and a limited amount of fun.

All this structure has another unintended consequence. Author Jay Coakley addresses adult influence in his book, *Sport in Society*:

> We have all heard horror stories about the extreme behaviors of some "little league parents" and insensitive, win-oriented coaches. Fortunately, these stories describe only a minority of the adults connected with organized teams and leagues. Most parents and coaches have good intentions. They do not try to make children unhappy and miserable. However, they do make mistakes. And one of the most frequent mistakes is to expect their children and their teams to act like miniature versions of adults and adult teams. (Coakley, p. 114)

All of us well-intentioned grownups want the kids to build and enhance their abilities and self-confidence on these wonderful facilities with all this great gear (and our fantastic guidance). But it can create just the opposite outcome. It often fosters a lack of internal motivation and drive. The overpowering and controlling organizational structure creates an environment where the player can avoid taking responsibility for individual performance, either good or bad. It becomes convenient to blame those "in control" for faults and flaws. It's easy to say those (bad) coaches just don't understand. Kids can also blame their parents for not getting the uniforms washed, for not getting the kid to a practice or a game on time, and so on. These sentiments easily lead to the negative results of:

▲ Low personal expectations
▲ Diminished desire to win
▲ Low drive
▲ Less desire to have fun
▲ Low levels of involvement

Providing additional thoughts on highly structured games, Jay Coakley says:

> Could it be that the well-meaning attempts to give children ready-made activities to fill their leisure time have backfired? Are the children who live in leisure-rich industrial countries growing up without learning how to organize their own games? Can't these children play games in which they don't have the assistance of referees, uniforms, coaches, and time clocks? (Coakley, p. 118)

Informal unstructured pickup games are actually great practices geared for fun. Unfortunately, we see less and less of these types of games. In the minds of the kids, sports have turned from being fun kid-controlled activities to events controlled by grownups. Kids don't play when they "want to" anymore. They "have to" play or practice when the scheduled time arrives. Sure, they all have the opportunities and facilities available to conduct their own pickup games, but they have less desire to organize their own pickup activities when they've already been practicing for long periods of time or are playing many structured games per week.

We can see the complexion of youth sports has changed. How we react to this new world of ours and conduct our activities will be critical to the enjoyment of everyone involved. And another factor in this whole gambit of youth sports is the parents. The next chapter takes a look at various parental types, their motivations, and their influences.

Chapter Highlights
to Improve Your Game Plan

▲ Unstructured pick-up games have been replaced with formal organized practices and games.

▲ Kids have lost the feelings of control because adults have taken over.

▲ Well-intentioned adults have created an environment that steals internal motivation and responsibility from the kids.

CHAPTER 5

Parents

Many different kinds

Newspapers all across this nation display headlines about parents and their horrid behavior. Parents scream at the coaches. They yell at their own kids. They insult other kids. Verbal and physical fights break out. Coaches and umpires have been attacked, even killed. No youth sport is immune from this potentially destructive behavior. And we dare to call this "recreation"? Jay Coakley gives us additional insights about parent involvement:

> It is quite possible that organized children's athletics has had as large an impact on family structure and behavior as any other societal event in the past three decades. However, we must be careful not to jump to the conclusion that whenever parents and children are involved in something together, they get along in positive ways. Some parents act in ways that can damage their relationships with their children. When parents become too emotionally involved in organized youth sports, their behavior often overwhelms and creates anxiety for their children. (Coakley, p. 116)

There's on old saying, "The best team to coach is from an orphanage." We know that every situation or parent group is not this bad, but the phrase makes a point. Parents can be great fans and offer good team support. Parents can also become a negative and destructive force that team coaches have to deal with. Let's look at some considerations we all must be aware of as coaches working with young athletes and their parents. As a parent, if you find yourself in any of the negative categories, please remember the games are for the benefit of the kids involved, and you should adjust your behavior accordingly.

Categories

There's a wide variety of parents all coaches must keep in mind. Usually our seasons go pretty smoothly, but every year we find ourselves in situations with parents we would rather not be in. It's times like these we must remind ourselves why we are involved in youth sports to begin with. Every coach or parent can identify with some of the "unique" people outlined in this chapter. Here are the main types of parents we all encounter.

Vicarious Villains

These people are usually ex-jock wannabees. Often they were not athletes in school or as a youth. Maybe they had to work for money so they could not participate in the limited offerings of school sports. Maybe they had good potential and ability but never realized that potential. Or maybe they were poor athletes and they know it, and that knowledge has always bothered them. Now that these parents have kids, they'll try to make sure their kid does not suffer the same lack of participation they did. Many of these vicarious villains want to relive some positive aspect (or negative avoidance) of their own youth through their young child. Living vicariously is natural and simply enjoying what a child is doing is healthy as long as the parent's involvement does not come at the expense of the child. If these types of parents cannot see success in their own lives and feel successful only if their child is successful, it is way too much pressure to dump on a young person.

You can easily identify these ex-jock vicarious villains. They spend countless hours discussing their child's sport. They wear sports jerseys and jackets of their favorite teams. They become consumed with sports and their child's athletics become the center-piece of their lives.

Quiet and Supportive

Coaches love these parents. They try to attend all games. Their primary goal is to be present for their child and to watch their child participate. They want to support the coach and the kids in any way they can. Their behavior is positive and they fit the classic definition of a good fan and spectator. As coaches, we have a thousand things we're trying to do before, during, and after a game. Dealing with parents is not one of our priorities. Polite supportive parents realize their role is secondary to the goals of their kids and are always welcome at games and competitive events. We like these parents. In their book, *Parents as Mentors*, Sandra Burt and Linda Perlis write:

> Parents provide encouragement by our investment of time, energy, and sometimes money for practice, play, coaching, training, equipment, special clothing, or entrance fees. Children thrive on the camaraderie of their teammates, but their most significant support begins at home. (Burt and Perlis, p. 184)

Jekyll and Hyde

Most people are solid members of their community. They're usually positive individuals, and we'd normally say they are nice people to be around when we meet them on the street. But for some parents, when it involves their own kid playing in a particular sport, look out. You never know which parent will turn into this dreaded sports monster. But we have all seen the normally pleasant John and Mary Doe transform his or her entire personality. They grow hair on the palms of their hands and their pleasant personal smiles turn into mean verbal assaults against coaches, umpires, and even their own kids. And when the game is over, they turn back into the nice person we thought we all knew.

Guilty Givers

In today's society, many fathers are absent from the lives of their kids because of an overemphasis on career or marital status situations. Many moms work outside the home. When these parents see other parents actively attending games, it is easy to feel guilty. To make sure their kids know they really care and to share in their experiences, they may overcompensate by becoming extremely vocal or over-involved. There is a time and a place for parental involvement. Parents can have wonderful influences as they help mold their own children psychologically. On the other hand, there are definite times, like during a game, that their role should be limited. They help the team and the players if they are seen and not heard. Guilt-ridden parents lose the proper perspectives of youth sports. After all, these are youth sports involving young people, not parental sports.

Ax Grinders

Some parents are upset from day one. They don't like your practice schedule because it interferes with their personal activities or other engagements. They don't agree with your style or practice/game formats. They could be upset with you for unknown reasons. Maybe this type of parent doesn't like the way the teams are structured or chosen. Who knows? Whatever the reason, this parent tends to be rude and can be explosive. Some also have no problem voicing their negative opinions to other parents and spectators. You can always identify these types of parents because of their nonstop criticism and complaining. They have a hard time simply enjoying the activity their child has chosen to participate in.

Know-It-Alls

These parents believe they alone know everything there is to know about a sport. They constantly offer unsolicited advice on practice formats and game strategies. They have plenty of constructive criticism to "help" us. They'll give us advice pertaining to their own kid as well as other kids on the team. In their minds they are trying to help, so we always have to walk a fine line with this type of parent. Usually, over time, these parents reduce their "help" as we demonstrate control of the team in our own way with our other coaches.

Absentee Parents

This parent is simply not involved in the chosen sport of their child at all. They don't transport him or her to practices and games. They don't do much in the way of washing any uniforms. We don't see them at games in support of their child. Maybe these parents want the sporting activity to remain in the control of the kids and are afraid of interfering. Maybe they realize they fit one of the previous negative categories so they stay away. Maybe they realize youth sports should be only for kids. Maybe they just don't care. It's hard to tell.

With all these types of parents, we'll have the potential for problem situations. Chapter 20 is dedicated to dealing with and heading off these problems.

Parental Motivations

Different things motivate different parents to be involved in youth sports. Let's take a look at the major motivational factors that dictate why parents do the things they do in the name of "helping my child."

Late Starters

These are usually adults who got married in their late thirties or forties and are well established in their jobs, careers, and lifestyles. They often have more disposable income and can afford to buy their kids the best gear, the best shoes, etc. Many late starters are motivated by competition with other parents. For many years, at the workplace, or within their own circle of acquaintances, late starters have heard all the stories of kids in youth sports. These late starters want to make sure their own kids get the best possible opportunities.

Want the Best

Most parents can be classified as wanting the best for their child. In today's society with all the potentially negative forces kids are exposed to, these parents want their kids involved in positive activities. The motivation for these parents is understandable and commendable. Parents in this category are great to have around if

31

they control themselves and if they behave in positive, supportive ways. Every one of us probably fits this category of adult motivation. We all have good intentions and ultimately, we all have the potential to positively impact our kids.

Support Versus Pushing

It is a good thing when a parent shows positive support toward their child's activity. The young athlete is more apt to practice and improve and enjoy him- or herself. The opposite type of parent aggressively pushes their child to be involved, usually in a sport the parent prefers. This obviously leads to kids not enjoying the activity. Kids may go through the motions physically, but their hearts and souls will not be in the sport. Author Barbara Meltz, in *Put Yourself in Their Shoes,* writes:

> While parents may hope their extracurricular dollars are giving their child an edge, the opposite may be true. Research shows that children who start an activity, especially a sport, at an early age are more likely to drop out in middle or high school than if they had started it at a later age. They burn out. In addition, there are decided disadvantages to a child's having too many activities. They become over programmed. Without time to just be a kid and play, they don't know how to relax and veg out. Studies show that imagination and creativity suffer. (Meltz, p.171)

Pushing a child into a particular sport creates negative outcomes. Not all kids are superior athletes. Being pushed by their parents sends a bad message to the kids. It can set up the child for ridicule and lead to feelings of false success. Kids know instinctively if they play well or not. Of course, youth sports are a good avenue for learning and gaining skill. But if a child believes he or she performs poorly at a particular sport and is forced to participate, they will not attain the positive effects of self-confidence and pleasure. Being forced to participate in a sport where they cannot perform contradicts the desired goals of fun and friendship.

32

Social Activity

We've all seen parents motivated by the social aspect of the game. Of course, they are motivated to watch their kids, but a strong secondary motivation is the additional benefit of social interaction. They stand or sit on the sidelines or in the bleachers spending much of the game socializing and conversing. They sometimes have no idea of what is going on in the game and often don't know the score. These parents love to congregate, catch up on all the latest news, and often just be with other parents and friends.

Bragging Rights

Parents in this category all seem to fit a certain mold. They just love to tell anyone within earshot about their kid. Pride is one thing, but these parents go way overboard and can't wait to brag about the latest great play their kid made.

"Make-Me-Look-Good"

For many parents, their own self-image and feeling of individual self-worth are tied directly to the performance of their child. This performance can be in the area of academics, music, social success, sports, etc. Talk about unnecessary negative pressure! Parents in this category (and even some coaches) need to reassess their own motivations and develop a better perspective of youth sports in general. This is an unhealthy form of motivation and can only lead to heartache and sadness. It's natural for all parents to gain pleasure from their children's accomplishments. But we've all seen parents without a solid foundation in their own lives. They live through the activities of their kids and ultimately harm themselves and the very kids they truly believe they're helping. A healthy perspective is important. Chapter 26 will deal with gaining a proper perspective.

Involvement

Usually, coaches don't have to interact much with parents harboring negative personalities or motivations. Other parents and fans are the people who must tolerate all categories of parents. Coaches can't change basic human nature, especially in adults. As a result, an individual coach will usually have minimal impact on parent types or their motivations. Because time is limited, a coach's job is primarily focused on the kids.

Hopefully, coaches get a group of players with parents who fit into the positive supportive categories. We coaches rarely hear or even see these parents. They simply, with good loving intentions, want their sons or daughters to be with other kids. They want their kids to improve in all the social skills that are so critical for later years. These parents also want their children to build basic self-confidence and esteem, and to have an enjoyable and satisfying experience. If these simple goals sound somewhat familiar, they should. These are the same goals we as coaches all have for the kids who are loaned to us.

Chapter Highlights
to Improve Your Game Plan

▲ Parents can be positive or negative as they become more and more involved in youth sports.

▲ Parents come in many personality types and have a variety of motivations (some helpful and some harmful).

CHAPTER 6

Coaches

Unique personalities and motivations

There are many different kinds of coaches with many different personalities. Some are passive and easygoing. Nothing seems to get them excited. Some are aggressive and remind spectators of the notoriously famous World War II leader, General George Patton, yelling orders at his troops before going into battle. Many coaches have quiet voices that kids can barely hear. Others have mega-voices resembling foghorns in the dark of night. The great thing about these different coaching personalities is that they all can be effective as they work with kids. Some naturally focus on the inside of each player whereas others have to work at it and develop this important ability. There is no perfect mold for the "perfect" coach. It does not exist. There are as many types of coaches as there are different youth sporting activities. But there is one skill every coach should understand and adopt: Every coach is responsible for his or her personal behavior and must willingly accept the awesome responsibility to mold every young person in positive ways. Regardless of his or her sport and individual style or personality, any coach can learn how to coach from the inside out—and benefit from it.

The Extremes

Before we examine the different categories of coaches, let's visualize two coaching styles found on opposite ends of the coaching spectrum. You will recognize specific traits in coaches you know, or perhaps in yourself.

The first example demonstrates a coach who despite positive intentions does not understand or implement the many great opportunities that can benefit the kids. This coach wants to eliminate all pressure from the kids. Practices are kept to a minimum because they are misunderstood as too hard or perhaps unnecessary to achieve the coach's goal. This goal is usually for the kids to participate in the sport regardless of any individual or team performance level. The coach considers all players to be equal and every young athlete receives equal playing time during game situations. Usually under this coaching philosophy, players rotate at various positions freely without regard to their individual talents. The coach in our example proudly proclaims his or her philosophy of equal participation to all players and parents.

Here are the negative outcomes and missed golden opportunities that result from this type of coach. First, there is a diminished emphasis on repetitive practice drills and therefore limited physical and mental improvement. There is also minimal time spent together at practices, which eliminates positive team-building activities. The kids don't get to know others on their team or their coaches. If a coach lets everyone receive equal playing time during actual games, he or she eliminates a basic childhood motivation factor. This factor is rooted in the belief that if a player works hard to attain a higher level of performance, he or she will be rewarded with key playing positions or get to start the game. If kids are all treated equally, regardless of actual levels of talent, they lose their natural incentive to improve. Above-average kids will feel slighted and not enjoy the activity. Below-average kids will have no desire to improve because they'll get equal playing time regardless of their skills.

Teams that play under this coaching philosophy often have poor win/loss records. The entire emphasis is on participation and equality. There is little emphasis on playing competitively or striving to win. Throughout the game season, continuous losses take much of the joy out of the activity. Kids begin to lose their desire to participate and may not even return for the next season. They didn't sign up to win every game, but they didn't necessarily sign up to lose most every game either.

Now let's jump to the other end of the spectrum. This is the coach who focuses on winning, period. In Chapter 9, the entire philosophy of "win at all costs" is covered in detail. We'll mention it here only to show it's opposite results when compared to the coach who focuses only on equality. Often, the coach who values only winning talks the talk to his or her team. Parents are "told" that this type of coach truly cares for each individual player. The coach might present him- or herself very well in early meetings and make claims of fairness. But during game situations, especially those with close scores, this type of coach violates his or her own statements. Every action by the coach is geared to only one thing, winning. Nothing else matters. Key players get all the playing time. Emotional levels run high. Feelings get hurt. Kids begin to feel excessive negative pressure. This coach might have spoken the right words on the outside, but on the inside, the single dominant motivation is on the final score. This inconsistency sends mixed signals to the players and their parents.

As we will show throughout the rest of this book, our goal should be somewhere between the two extremes. Coaches should have solid fun practices to teach and elevate the development of every player. They should spend much time with their team to develop the mental attitudes of confidence, proper perspective, and motivation. Good coaches motivate all the kids to strive to do their best and get them involved in the game. Kids should learn the important value of practicing and improving. Then they should be rewarded for their effort, their favorable performance, and their positive attitudes.

Please keep the above examples of extreme coaches in mind as you read the additional thoughts and considerations in the rest of this chapter.

Parents as Coaches

With the huge variety of sporting activities today, there are many different avenues for parents to participate in some kind of coaching role. Today many dads and moms are getting involved as coach volunteers, helping out the team with other interested adults. They start early as their kids begin in sports.

When parents who are relatively new to the sport and all its intricacies get involved, there is a strong positive outcome. This situation avoids the jock syndrome where an ex-jock incorrectly assumes he or she will automatically make a good coach. If these neophyte coaches are smart enough to realize how little they know about coaching teams of young people, they usually are more receptive to learning as much as they can. It is incumbent upon parent coaches to learn proper basic skills as best they can. At every bookstore there are books available on the technical aspects of particular sports. Also, libraries carry instructional books and videotapes on specific sports. Parents and coaches should review these materials and learn the basics about their sport. They should also listen and learn from other coaches already involved in youth sports. Often, sporting organizations will offer youth coach clinics and training toward certification. Most importantly, every coach should learn and practice the principles found in this book of properly developing young people from the inside out. A skilled coach will constantly try to learn as much as possible. All coaches will make mistakes. Good coaches will learn from them.

Finally, coaches should strive to make practices both fun and educational. Later in this book you'll find a typical practice format that can be tailored to the specific ages of your young athletes. Through trial and error, coaches should experiment and try different techniques to reach success. The key is to be patient and have an open mind to all avenues of improvement. Becoming a good coach does not happen overnight.

Dedicated Adults

Coaches in this broad category are often longtime residents in a community with a vested interest in the long-term positive growth of individual boys and girls and local youth sports in general. These adults are usually part of an organization or school. Local groups and associations count on volunteer coaches to assist in the development of community teams. Many of these dedicated coaches have had a child of their own involved in earlier years but now do it for the overall good of many kids.

Frequently there are many dedicated people "behind the scenes" of successful organizations. The world is filled with truly good people with big hearts and a willingness to offer their help, especially if it benefits our young people. Our sporting programs and our kids often benefit from the hard work of these individuals. We owe them our gratitude.

Ex-Jocks

Many times we see coaches who were at one time active young athletes themselves. This presents potential advantages and disadvantages. Advantages include coaches who have solid sports knowledge. They know game situation strategies and have a strong overall background. They have "been there" and know the game.

There are also some disadvantages with many ex-jocks. Some think they know everything there is to know about the game. They don't watch the latest in coaching training videos or read the current instructional books. They don't realize coaching is different from just playing. There are many adults who were good athletes when they were kids but make terrible coaches. There are also many great coaches who did not play organized youth sports. The key is to develop a long-term quest for knowledge and improvement.

Teachers as Coaches

In communities all across the country many teachers also perform as youth coaches. Schoolteacher coaches rarely have their own child in the sport they coach. As a teacher, being a coach is an extra responsibility above and beyond normal classroom education. Regarding financial reimbursement, many get paid for the time dedicated to coaching. Many others do not. If paid, regardless of actual time logged in, we all know coaching takes countless hours of planning and organizing the many aspects of youth sports. Whether we are paid or not, our reimbursement for being a coach usually does not come in the form of money, but in our own self-awareness of the positive role we play with the young people we work with.

Kids as Coaches

Team members often can have a positive role as an assistant coach or team captain. They must have the respect of the other players and strong game knowledge. Not every team can benefit from a player helping with the coaching responsibilities. But if you do decide to try enlisting the help of a young athlete for this special team position, there are a few options to consider.

One alternative is to have the team elect a captain. But beware of a popularity contest. Instruct the team to choose a captain with qualities consistent with "middle management" leadership abilities. The elected captain must be able to organize and implement basic team requirements, such as pregame warm-up exercises, practice drills, team communications, and other tasks. A team captain must have a willingness and ability to give instructions. Coaches will often rely on the team captain to act as an assistant coach.

Another option is to appoint a team captain early in the season or midway into the season. In most cases you will receive better results in the long-term development of the team if you select the correct team captain yourself. You'll have to decide this on your own depending on your team's situation. A good strategy to motivate the team is to partially hand the reins over to a team captain (or co-captains). If done properly, in the spirit of allowing the team to take control of its own destiny, this can be a tremendous team enhancement. In Chapter 22, which covers mid-season motivational adjustments, a scenario utilizing this technique is explained in greater depth.

Psycho-Coach

These coaches lose their overall perspective and forget why youth sporting activities exist. All coaches give much time and energy to the game. But the psycho-coach becomes over-involved and transfers him- or herself into the game. This coach lives like a young athlete and participates in all the drills. They mentally lose the distinction between themselves and the players. This becomes a problem if the coach uses players like pawns on his or her own chessboard of life. Obviously a coach's main interest should be the athlete. But if athletes are treated as objects for a psycho-coach's personal ego and goals, they will feel resentment and ultimately these kids will suffer. Avoid becoming this type of coach.

Whatever the individual coaching style or personality, we can all agree that as coaches we have a profound impact on kids. They learn more about life from their combined experiences with all their coaches than they realize. As coaches, we know the many lessons they learn and it is often our inner knowledge of long-term helpfulness that keeps us active and involved.

CHAPTER 7

Time Competition

Kids get pulled in so many directions

As adults in society, we have created an environment for ourselves that is full of schedules, clocks, deadlines, dates, and appointments. Everything seems structured. In many ways, we have transferred our hectic lifestyles to our younger generation. It seems like every child must carry a pocket computer or calendar to schedule his or her many appointments. It is sad that today, many factors compete for the limited "spare" time available to our youth. As coaches and as parents, we must be aware of the many influences that kids deal with on a daily basis. The true time we have with any individual player or team can be limited and we must utilize that precious time to its maximum benefit. This chapter highlights the primary activities that compete with us for a child's time.

Video World

Wow! How do we even compare today's barrage of video images hitting our kids' senses to the limited video opportunities of long ago? Today kids have exposure to:

▲ Playstation and Playstation 2

▲ Xbox

▲ Nintendo 64
▲ Big screen TV
▲ Rental movies for VCRs and DVD players
▲ Computers
▲ 50-plus TV channels
▲ TVs in their bedrooms
▲ And more!

Academics

Schools and educational pressures of today pull at a child's available time. In many areas we are seeing variable length school days, some with earlier start times and some with prolonged ending times. The demands of homework also exist. Overall there is a strong push for good grades that requires dedicated attention to classroom activities.

Jobs

Many young athletes also have jobs that consume their time. They work for money to upkeep and maintain their consumer-related lifestyles. There are requirements for home chores as well as formal outside work. Depending on the ages of the kids, they can work anywhere from 3 to 15 hours per week or more. Just think what kind of athletes they could be if they practiced a fraction of this time. Just a thought.

Multiple Sports

There are many sporting options available to kids today. They can choose from a smorgasbord of different competitive opportunities throughout the entire year. Kids are encouraged to participate in many sports. Parents want their kids to test many activities to get a wide sampling of likes and dislikes.

Miscellaneous Activities

Aside from the many competing athletic options today's kids have, there are also many other choices. Here are just some of the more common alternatives of time competition:

▲ Overlapping sports activities
▲ Computer time and e-mail communications
▲ Boy Scouts and Girl Scouts
▲ Music lessons
▲ Future Farmers of America
▲ Hanging out with friends
▲ Religious youth groups
▲ Boyfriends and girlfriends
▲ Hunting
▲ 4-H groups
▲ Sleeping in
▲ Phone conversations
▲ Dance lessons
▲ Plus many more after-school and weekend activities

Family

The average school year lasts nine months. During the year, kids have practices and games after school and well into the evenings. There are also many summer sporting options. These activities tend to cut into one of the long-term keys to family development. This key is having dinner and conversation together as a family. Spending time with the family is as important today as it ever has been. Families need time to enjoy vacations and weekends together whenever possible. There are many negative forces that face kids today and a strong family influence will keep them on the proper course through their teen years. Coaches need to be aware of this critical form of time competition and its long-term importance to every child. It is sometimes easy for coaches to be selfish and want much of a child's time but ultimately, a solid family life is more important than a sports team.

Team Fundraisers

Money drives many aspects of today's organized sports. It is used for tournaments, uniforms, facilities improvements, gear and equipment, trophies and awards, and team recognition celebrations. As we can see by all the other forces competing for the limited time of a young athlete, practicing and playing a particular sport gets harder and harder. On top of all this, coaches often want the team to be heavily involved in various fundraisers. Every coach must ponder an important question and determine if this is the best way to utilize the small ration of time these kids allocate to their chosen sport. We coaches want to instill some appreciation into the kids for all the goodies they have in youth sports. But maybe with a little creativity (and more parental involvement) money could be raised for the kids but without so much time required from each athlete. Just a few alternate possibilities include finding local business sponsor(s) or simply asking local businesses for contributions.

Kid Leisure Time

We cannot overlook this important necessity. Kids need some physical and mental downtime in today's hectic world. Barbara Meltz also writes:

> They have activity piled upon activity. They are pushed and pulled every which way, taught to squeeze meaning into every minute. As soon as they are old enough to tell time, children are taught to live by it. (Meltz, p. 175)

Today's kids are the victims of a "hurry-up society" with many activities. Many kids also have parents who are constantly busy and in a hurry. There are too many pressures on kids to grow up quickly. Kids need to just be kids. They need their own downtime and we need to let them just be relaxed and lazy from time to time. In this vein, have you as a coach ever thought of setting up some downtime activity unrelated directly to your sport? Maybe you could organize a team event in the park, or a trip to a professional or semi-professional sporting event. Maybe you could have an informal activity at someone's home. Be creative. This form of organized laziness could pay some great unexpected dividends in the areas of team unity, friendship development, and plain old fun. Lamenting lost childhoods, Barbara Meltz offers:

There can be times in the life of a child when a little bore-dom is a good thing. This gets back to all that structure we're constantly putting into their lives. There can be so much that we rob them of the chance to be creative and spontaneous in their play, to daydream and stare at the sky. Our children are growing up learning that only a pro-grammed, goal-oriented activity is worth doing. The joy of childhood is getting lost in our busy world. (Meltz, p. 184)

Chapter Highlights
to Improve Your Game Plan

▲ Regardless of the individual coaching personality, every coach can mold kids from the inside out.

▲ At one end of the spectrum, some coaches focus on equal participation and ignore physical and mental preparation.

▲ At the other end of the spectrum, many coaches focus excessively on winning with no regard to the individual player.

▲ There are many factors competing for the time of today's kids.

▲ Major activities include the video world, academics, jobs, other sports, family responsibilities, fund raisers, and lei-sure time.

INTERMISSION

Most sports have periodic breaks that offer time to regroup before continuing. From time to time, it's healthy to stretch our legs and our minds. This short page is our "break in the action."

Before we go any further, let's quickly recap. Chapters 1, 2, and 3 reminded us of the good old days of youth sports. Those were simpler times. Chapters 4 through 7 have shown us where we are today and what we as coaches and parents have to deal with. Now it's time to sit back and open your mind because we are going to embark on a new journey. We're going deep inside the mind, the psyche, and the inner person of a young athlete. You will not be subjected to psychological theories or 10-dollar analytical words. Instead, you will be offered common-sense English descriptions of the important topics that are necessary for you to understand and then implement effective guidance from the inside out. There is no single across-the-board formula for every coaching style with every team for every sport. Nor is every parent alike. We are all a continuous work-in-progress and my goal is to get us all thinking about how we can help our young athletes.

The rest of this book is the meat and potatoes of the entire platter. If practiced year after year, it will help the young people you guide and enhance your personal enjoyment. As you read on, please open your mind and think about how the general points and ideas in the following chapters apply to you and your children. Highlight those key points or thoughts that will best help you appreciate being a positive coaching or parenting influence. After all, we cannot forget, this is supposed to be fun for us too

SECTION III

Inside

Notes and Thoughts

CHAPTER 8

The Individual Player

What makes him or her tick?

What is a youth? What goes on inside their minds and bodies and hearts? What makes them tick and how do we connect in a positive beneficial way? First and foremost, a youth is self-centered and believes the universe revolves around him or her. They have a strong "me/I" focus. Their view of life is in a tiny world, not expanded fully as it is for adults. Their perspective is small and they exist within their own little comfort zone boundaries.

By nature young people are self-absorbed. As we all know, few naturally take responsibility for their actions, inactions, improvements, lack of improvement, performance, etc. With a young athlete (and most older ones) their entire life focus can be summed up in one acronym: WIIFM. What's in it for me? This is their dominant driving thought. They approach everything from this mental perspective. This self-focus is natural and eventually becomes expanded as part of the overall normal maturation process. In *Stress and Your Child*, Bettie Youngs states:

> When children are very small, their world centers on themselves. Everything is *me! I want! Mine!* We laugh and indulge

the toddlers, but soon we begin teaching them that there are other people who have rights, too, that they need to share and be part of the larger scene. (Youngs, p. 55)

Most kids outgrow this self-focus and eventually begin to think of others' thoughts and feelings. But in the meantime, kids need to know what's in it for them. They participate in sports for fun and they don't like being forced to do anything just for the sake of doing it. They need to understand why. And once they understand the rationale and accept it, their own level of desire grows. Side note: Unfortunately we all know some so-called "grownups" who have not gone through this process of perspective expansion. Hopefully not many of these "grownups" are in the position of a youth sports coach.

So what does this youth self-focus mean to us? How do we coaches deal with so many kids wondering, "What's in it for me?" First we have to realize that we are in the tremendous yet difficult position of interacting with many maturity levels at one time. Add to this the various factors that affect kids when they show up for a practice or a game. They deal with pre-puberty, relationship problems with friends, puberty, arguments at home, post-puberty, etc. How do we work our magic in this crazy environment? It's virtually impossible to work closely with each individual player in any great detail. There's not enough time in the day. But we coaches can have a general overall awareness of what goes on inside the players' minds and bodies. We must stay above the normal expected petty youth situations by maintaining our focus on the mental aspects of the sport and encouraging each player to do his or her best.

As parents, our primary responsibility in life is to properly guide and raise our children into adulthood. Every parent can understand the multitude of individual personalities a coach must deal with throughout a given season. You might also recognize some of the following traits within your own kids and work to positively influence individual attitudes and behaviors.

What an opportunity for people like us. We have all these wild-eyed basket cases who don't realize they're wild-eyed basket cases. Worse yet, they think that all coaches, all parents, all teachers, and all grownups have no concept of reality. As we accept this challenge, we can help these young people who are yearning for a place in life to develop some basic desirable human traits, like doing one's best, confidence, and teamwork. But first, let's identify some typical categories of kids. Then we'll look at what drives and motivates the kids we mold.

Types of Players

The Natural

Every coach has experienced this type of player. They are the superstars in their neighborhood, in the school, and on the team. They can be a tremendous asset to the team if channeled properly. Certainly they help with their high skill levels in game situations. But they also can be excellent candidates for a team captain position. It depends on the person. A potential drawback to the natural athlete could be that he or she does not have to work as hard as others to be "good." Our job is to challenge and develop each player regardless of their ability to improve and achieve beyond their individual limitations. One player's "best" is another player's mediocrity. We must expect the best performance from each, regardless of natural ability. Everyone can improve above and beyond his or her current level. In her book, *Dr. Sylvia Rimm's Smart Parenting*, Dr. Rimm writes:

> Children who succeed all the time or who get all A's effortlessly are not prepared for a competitive society. They've learned to function only in a world without challenge. Their self-confidence is dependent on being first, perfect, at the top, and always winning. When they find themselves in situations where they're somewhat less successful, second best, or surrounded by other extremely intelligent people, they may feel like failures. Their confidence falters dramatically, and they may feel defeated or depressed. If they've learned to function in competition, they reset their goals, view their failure as a temporary setback, and persevere. (Rimm, p. 276)

Cocky

The cocky player struts around the field or diamond and has quite a self-important attitude. It can be easy for coaches to not enjoy having this young person on the team. There are two types of cocky player. One is the natural athlete with an attitude. The other is someone without extraordinary ability but with an arrogant attitude nonetheless. Both types can be positive additions to the team if they adopt the proper team attitude. That's where our good coaching skills come in. It's our job to focus on the team aspect of the sport and remind all players that every game depends on solid team play, not a bunch of individuals.

Head Case

These players are tough to figure out because there can be so many causes to their emotional state. Maybe they show off. Maybe they are moody. Maybe they're having problems at home or at school. Sometimes they're great to have around while sometimes they're a big pain. As coaches we must be aware that these players exist and try to treat them like the others on the team.

100 Percent Desire

Coaches love these players. Usually they are quieter kids. They focus internally and their goal is to give 100 percent effort all the time. Some want to practice and play to their highest level. Some are driven by other motives. Whatever the reason, other players can learn from the 100 percent desire players and adopt their good attitude, behavior, and commitment.

The Mouth/Comedian

When we coaches talk to the team it's because we have something the team needs to hear and learn. The mouth/comedians sometimes decide they need to talk while the coach talks. They can be rude and disruptive. This person obviously stands out early and needs to be silenced immediately. Chapter 12 deals with discipline and the mouth/comedian player is easily handled using some common-sense techniques found in that chapter.

Junior Pro In Training

All kids dream of the "big leagues" and the "big money." There are also parents out there harboring professional aspirations for their little athlete. Often the pressure on this fast track is unbearable. Parents and coaches alike must analyze their own motivations to be sure they are doing what's best for the child athlete. To set the record straight, here are some numbers. In his book, *Sports Without Pressure*, author Eric Margenau provides thought-provoking statistics:

> There are more than two million high school athletes. Out of that pool of two million athletes, the country's colleges give athletic scholarships to an estimated 20,000 young men and women. After three or four years of competition, several thousand of these athletes, both the good and the very good, have dropped out of contention for the pros or the Olympics because of injury, a decision to play out the college string and not go on, plans for further schooling, a loss of interest during their college years, or a realization that, compared to their peers, they really don't have the talent to go any further. Nevertheless, a good number of college athletes (as many as 10,000 each year) continue to harbor the dream of a professional career and pursue that dream with vigor. Upon graduation, they have high hopes that a sports career lies ahead of them.

> Most of those dreams are quickly shattered, simply because there are not enough places to work. In this country, there are roughly 2,000 jobs available in the four major spectator sports of baseball, football, basketball, and hockey. There are approximately 500 more spots in tournament time golf and tennis, and a few more in soccer, ice skating, and running. So if we're generous we can say there are 3,000 people who are bona fide professional athletes, that is, people whose primary job is performing in front of the public. Of these, 1,500 or so earn a lot of money, another 500

earn substantial money, and the rest earn a living. But that's not the whole story.

There may be 3,000 potential jobs overall, but each year there are only a few positions available on any given team and fewer jobs still on the tennis and golf circuit. The worlds of international gymnastics, track and field, ice skating, and soccer add only a handful more jobs to the pool. (Margenau, p. 87)

As a result, a young athlete's odds of turning into a professional are very low, regardless of his or her ability.

Inner Drive

Individual motivation and drive come in many shapes and forms. Here are a few general reasons kids are driven to participate in youth sports. Some kids have an older brother or sister who played the same sport. These kids are driven to fill some imaginary shoes or performance levels. Some strive for individual excellence. They practice hard at home on their own and with the team. These players get internal rewards for improving and doing well. Other players are driven by the desire for recognition from their friends and peers, members of the opposite sex, or their parents. These kids pursue acceptance by outside entities and feel successful as a result. A drawback to many of the external considerations is that if there is no acceptance from outside, the athlete could feel unsuccessful for the wrong reasons. We must help kids adopt the proper attitudes and perspectives of internal success.

Some kids are simply pressured, often over-pressured, by their parents. This is an outside motivator and rarely results in the long-term positive inner drive we prefer to see in young athletes. And finally, kids are motivated by the simple need to be with friends and have fun. This is crucial to their lives, always has been, always will be. And there's that word "fun" again. At this point let's address and answer the question, "What is fun?"

Fun is a relative term and its meaning is different for individual kids and a child's age. There is an evolution of fun that all kids go through. For children from six to nine years of age, participation is based on a focus of having a good time. If kids truly have fun and many good experiences in this early phase of life, they will be more apt to continue in the sport and play in subsequent years. If the child happens to learn something or improve a specific skill, that is secondary and almost irrelevant to the child. They usually don't know it but improvement will lead to enhanced performance later on and corresponding enjoyment. But for now, the focus is on fun.

As a young person enters the age range of 10 to 14 years, he or she begins to shift the focus from pure 100 percent fun to a 50/50 combination of fun and other considerations. This other side of the fun equation includes conversation with friends, minimal hard work, and a minor growing emphasis on competition. After about 15 years of age, the fun scale becomes dominated by other areas. Fun changes. Kids begin to focus on individual improvement, team involvement, competition, and winning. Fun evolves into satisfaction and pride. It is reflected in a positive self-image and a feeling of increased self-worth. Fun grows into a belief of true accomplishment.

In the classic movie *Mary Poppins*, while preparing to clean the nursery, she says to the children, "there is an element of fun in every job (like practice) and if we (coaches and parents) find the fun, the job is a game." As coaches, it is our job to help kids believe hard work can be fun. We do this by blending repetitive work with positive fun, and later chapters will illustrate specific examples. Also, kids must learn that serious competition can be fun. Winning is fun and it's easy to have fun after a win, but to turn a loss into a fun experience is a big challenge. Individually, kids often get over the negative feelings of a loss in about 5 or 10 minutes (it usually takes us adults a little longer). Our job is to effectively use the short post-game time of being upset in a productive way. This is often easier said then done. A hard loss from serious competition may not appear to be "fun" at the moment, but good can be gained as a result of the loss.

Skillful coaching can help each young athlete learn some of life's valuable lessons. Immediately following a loss, a short time period of 5 or 10 minutes is a good time to reflect on areas for improvement as a team. With every loss, you will help each young athlete learn how to cope with losses and minor disappointments. The next chapter deals with this team psychology and team development and your critical part of the team equation.

Chapter Highlights
to Improve Your Game Plan

▲ Kids are "I" focused and always want to know what's in it for them.

▲ Different types of players include the natural athlete, the cocky athlete, the head case, and junior pros in training.

▲ Fun is a critical part of kids' games and their individual motivations.

CHAPTER 9

The Team

Uniting many individuals to create winners

In today's environment of structured sports, thousands of organizations exist to assist individual sporting teams. All these groups, recreation departments, associations, communities, and schools operate somewhat differently with different formats and ways of conducting their programs. But all have as their common goal the development of the program, the team, and those on the team. This is where we as coaches and parents come in. Author Karlene Sugarman writes about team development in her book, *Winning the Mental Way*:

> A team is a group of people who share common goals, a common vision and have some level of interdependence that requires both verbal and physical interaction. Teams come into existence through shared attitudes. They may come together for a number of different reasons, but their goals are the same—to achieve peak performance in their endeavors. (Sugarman, p. 31)

City, School, or Organization

In organized sports, rarely is a team on its own. They have strong histories of support (money and time) by one of the above-mentioned groups. There are long established traditions within all these organizations and any single team is just one in a long line of past and future teams. Every player needs to be aware of its sponsoring organization and have an idea of the "behind the scenes" support. It is important to instill a strong sense of pride in each team member. A great starting point and object of visible pride is the uniform. You should demand a high standard of uniform cleanliness and that it is worn properly at all times, to foster pride in the team and the organization. Many teams are the result of some kind of tryout format. Many others are chosen from large groups of kids who get split into competing teams. If the team is developed from tryouts, there is a pride that comes from "making the team." Regardless of how a team gets selected or developed, you can build pride and a sense of teamwork with uniforms and your consistent focus on a team philosophy. Karlene Sugarman writes:

> Each team functions within the image it has of itself—this is referred to as a self-fulfilling prophecy. If the team has the attitude that they are a confident and aggressive team, then they will portray that image on the outside by the way they carry themselves, and the way they feel about themselves on the inside. The team gets its image by way of uniforms/colors, mascot, team slogans, formations/rituals, and the interplay of the members. Gathering the team together before taking the field/court to call upon your slogan can help bond the team and enhance its confidence before entering the game. (Sugarman, p. 41)

Team Control

In general there are two broad categories of team control. The first is overt. It involves the use of rules and regulations. These are important so all players know and understand the boundaries of behavior. Overt control involves proper discipline and adherence to time demands. Overt control is the crucial teaching of standardized basics and skill mechanics.

The other form of team control is covert. This is more subtle and not easily seen by outsiders. Covert control is the toolbox by which we build individual players from the inside out. The covert tools of influence help us mold the attitudes and philosophies of players. We do our part to develop confident individual leaders and athletes. Covert coaching and guidance promote emotional motivation. They develop a sense of team unity and individual commitment to the team goals. The basic premise throughout most of this book works within this area of covert guidance and influence. Every parent and every coach can perform miracles in young people by utilizing the skills of covert influence.

"I" Versus "We"

Every kid is "I" focused. We as coaches or parents must blend this "I" focus with the "team" mentality. As coaches and parents, we certainly can recognize individual achievement and success. Feeling important enhances motivation and every player instinctively knows it takes many individuals to be a single team. We should, however, emphasize that the players win as a team and lose as a team. No single player can win or lose a game. We've all seen kids who would think differently, if we allowed it. In his book *Leading With the Heart*, author Mike Krzyzewski says:

> When it comes to my philosophy surrounding teamwork, I have a simple, straightforward saying that I pass on to anyone who will listen: Two are better than one if two act as one. And if you believe that two acting as one are better than one, just imagine what an entire team acting as one can do. (Krzyzewski, p. 83)

Our job is to communicate, instill, and reinforce the "team" philosophy early on. Each individual player needs to perform to the best of his or her ability. But at the end of the day, the team wins together or loses together. All players will have good and bad days, it's part of the game and part of life. We coaches must emphasize that all players need to be supportive of each other, especially if they're having one of those bad days. One behavior we cannot accept is negative critical comments from other players. This only leads to additional negative attitudes and behaviors. As parents and as coaches, we must instill the fact that every athlete at every level will have bad days. Dealing positively with failure and frustration is covered in detail in Chapter 11.

Winning Versus Excellence

Karlene Sugarman offers her insights on winning:

> Keep in mind, winning is not the only objective, it's more than that, it's the enhancement of your self-image and the fulfillment of your dreams. Winning has to be a personal thing of you achieving the goals that you have set for yourself. Don't lose sight of the fact that reaching a personal goal carries its own reward. It is overcoming any obstacles to reach your goal. The value of winning is only as great as the value of the goal you set and obtained. Real success is in your own mind, not in the minds of others. (Sugarman, p. 118)

There are two thought processes in place on how we as coaches approach a game. One is "win at all costs" and focuses on results. This philosophy creates a focus on the score instead of individual development. Author Shane Murphy, in his book *The Achievement Zone*, writes:

> Individuals with this orientation to competition are only happy when they are visibly successful. The result-focus approach to competition has a number of drawbacks. While people with this focus are keen to win, they won't risk new learning experiences if they think they might fail. This sharply limits their long-term improvement. Also, result-oriented athletes do their best only when they are evenly matched against their opposition. Against weaker opponents they tend to be over-confident, and against stronger opponents they tend to lack confidence. In both cases, their level of performance is not as good as it should be. (Murphy, p. 24)

Many coaches will ignore long-term physical mechanical improvement in place of short-term win/loss statistics if improving a physical skill means temporarily reducing a player's performance. Often a physical correction results in a reduction in performance until the skill becomes automatic (Chapter 15 details muscle memory). "Win at all costs" is a powerful attitude that creates negative pressure toward the wrong goals. This focus is on results and says the team can only be happy if they're ahead when the game ends. A focus on winning is also a focus on losing and there can only be one winner. When athletes (or coaches) focus on the result of winning, they only perform their best when they perceive similar abilities to their opponent. Our goal is to have our team and every individual achieve maximum performance levels, regardless of the opponent.

The second philosophy of youth sports is to "strive to win." This approach motivates players to practice and play their hardest and give 100 percent effort. This focus is based on action and instills the attitude of "striving to win," which is very different from "winning at all costs." Mike Krzyzewski also writes:

> A real winning attitude is about standards of excellence—which are variable from year to year, from team to team. Being the best you can be—and doing the best you can—are the constants. In building any winning team, it's important to remember that the members of the team don't have to be perfect; they just have to keep trying to be the best they can be. That's my definition of a winning attitude. (Krzyzewski, p. 28)

Athletes who focus on action try new improvements even if they make mistakes. We can foster an action-based focus and instill the belief that winning is execution. As coaches we can give constant positive feedback and positive constructive criticism. Our focus should be to communicate that every player can contribute to the team by giving 100 percent. They need to focus not on the opposing team, but rather on their own individual and team performance. These are the only parts of the game they can control.

Usually when a team loses, it is because they have beaten themselves. All we can ask is for each player to play his or her best. That is all they can ask of themselves. If they play their best they can walk off the field or diamond or court with their heads held high regardless of some short-term measurement called a "score." Having said all that, it won't take long for each child to learn that if they each perform their best individually and as a team, the team will usually win. Karlene Sugarman adds:

> If you play hard and smart, and focus on specific areas within your control, winning will take care of itself. When you are more concerned about the outcome than the process you are, ironically, decreasing your chances of seeing that happen. By keeping your focus on the process you are taking the emphasis off the outcome; and as a result, you will feel less pressure to win. (Sugarman, p. 117)

Be aware of a potential trap. Many adults will "talk the talk" and say they truly care about the team and want individuals to do their best. But we also must strive to "walk the talk." Our actions have to be consistent with our words and we need to reward individual success and improvement whenever possible. There's a big difference between saying "we're all winners if we just do our best" and "if we all do our best, we'll win the game." These will send a mixed message to your kids. The second phase shows too much emphasis on winning.

Team Building

Mike Krzyzewski offers this thought:

> When you first assemble a group, it's not a team right off the bat. It is a collection of individuals, just like any other group. And there is some truth to the adage "You're only as good as your talent." So assembling skillful individuals as part of your team is a given. Then, of course, it becomes a matter of motivating those people to perform as a team. (Krzyzewski, p. 22)

62

Just as kids grow from infancy to maturity, so do teams. As the new team comes together, players learn about one another and begin to get a feel for the group. They may try new things to test the waters and coaches. In these early stages, there's a lot to learn and each player begins to see where he or she fits in. All team goals and objectives also are made clear in this early phase. Coaches should discuss a variety of issues with the team. Examples include:

▲ Frequency of practices

▲ Coach's expectations

▲ Coach's philosophies

▲ Acceptable behavior and attitude

▲ Sportsmanship

▲ Absenteeism

▲ Rules

▲ Uniforms or other attire

▲ Transportation

▲ Schedules

▲ Do's and don'ts

▲ General introductions

▲ Open question-and-answer session

Team Unity

This phase of team development is evident with individuals searching for identity and a position within the team structure. Players exhibit true personalities and minor conflicts can occur. Conflicts stem from rivalries, jealousies, competition, egos, etc. Conflict is normal and must be addressed as soon as it appears. Unresolved conflict can result in resentment and added negativity within the group. The best way to deal with any conflict is to acknowledge it, identify a common ground, and look for the best solution. Team cohesion can actually increase after quick, fair, positive ends to conflict situations. How can you (covertly) build unity, self-direction, and team spirit? During the season encourage the team to play throughout the week on their own. They could have a scrimmage with no adults present. In the post season, encourage them to keep playing the sport. They'll actually be practicing but enjoying their own game.

Here's another idea you might want to try. We coaches all think we're important and our team couldn't operate without us. What would happen if we did not show up for a practice or a game? A little trick like this could force the players to think on their own and come together to make decisions. Maybe you could set it up with your other coaches and simply not show up for a practice. Make sure one player has the balls or other necessary gear and let the players run a practice on their own. This could be interesting. Maybe you could even watch (and learn) secretly from a distance (observing could also help avoid parent complaints of desertion). This could be an exercise in self-government. Obviously, this tactic must be age appropriate and used with sound judgment.

Team Success

The final stage of team development produces solid group attitudes and team member support. When all players work toward common outcomes, bonds of trust are formed. Individuals realize what it took to get this far and feel like they are part of something big. Players rise above their many differences and focus on the group's goals and objectives. All players know their roles and how they fit into the scheme of the group. Karlene Sugarman presents her thoughts on team unity:

> A cohesive team can be distinguished from a noncohesive team by many characteristics. A cohesive team has well-defined roles and group norms, common goals, a positive team identity, a good working relationship, shared responsibility, respect, positive energy, trust, a willingness to cooperate, unity, good communication, pride in membership, and synergy. (Sugarman, p. 55)

Keeping Score

To close this chapter, today's "no pressure, don't want to hurt their feelings" society has suggested youth sporting events should be played without keeping score. Overprotective, unrealistic parents and adults and their own misdirected beliefs drive this attitude. They believe we should shelter kids from the horrid experience of losing a game. Well, as we all know, kids will keep score regardless of whether we adults (in control of their game) formally keep it or not. Obviously an excessive focus on winning and a win-at-all-cost motivation are both bad.

But our goal is to strive to win. Kids know they compete for many reasons; one is winning. Winning and losing have tremendous value and benefits *if* we adults can effectively turn every win and loss into a learning opportunity and a lesson for life. Competition does not have to be a zero-sum game in which one side wins and one side loses. Obviously our culture places a high emphasis on winning. But competitive sports, even with scores kept, can be a positive-sum game in which both sides win, regardless of the score. Winning with sportsmanship and quiet nongloating confidence creates a person comfortable with winning and yet empathetic to losing. Losing creates a sense of humility and often creates an inner motivation to improve and do better the next time. Winners win games and lose games. Losing a game does not mean the team is filled with a bunch of losers. Winning and losing become an attitude.

Winning and losing are only a few of the integral components of the total sporting experience. For the kids under our care, our job is to help all players keep "winning" and "losing" in their proper perspective. The next several chapters will help us understand and positively teach these important philosophies.

Chapter Highlights
to Improve Your Game Plan

▲ In today's organized sporting world, there are many different local and national sporting organizations that sponsor teams.

▲ Covert influence can do miracles in the positive development of young athletes.

▲ Kids have a natural "I" focus that we must expand into a "team/we" focus.

▲ The philosophy of "striving to win" is superior to one of "win at all costs."

▲ Keeping score, winning, and losing are all important parts of youth sports (and of life).

CHAPTER 10

Pressure and Motivation

Starting with the positives

In the theater of your mind, imagine a young boy or girl involved in a competitive game situation. Time is running out and this young person finds him- or herself with a critical, highly visible opportunity. This is it. The game outcome could hinge on this one moment in time. Minds are racing. Coaches are yelling. Fans are cheering. Team members are encouraging. What an incredible emotionally charged moment. Try to imagine what might be going through the young person's mind. We're talking about pressure and its cousin, motivation. In *Winning the Mental Way*, Karlene Sugarman writes:

> Many times, you don't need a competitor or opposing team to beat you. You can do that all on your own by saying negative things to yourself while you are performing or playing a game. You can either be your own best friend or your own worst enemy—the choice is yours. It is very basic—positive self-talk will help your performance, negative self-talk will worsen it. (Sugarman, p. 171)

Pressure is a natural occurrence found in many circumstances throughout life, especially in competitive or visible situations. Pressure is a desirable characteristic if it is controlled. We play a major role in helping individuals and the team channel this pressure into an advantage that helps performance. Our job is to remove negative types of pressure and transfer feelings of anxiety into positive motivation. In her book, *From Panic to Power*, author Lucinda Bassett writes:

> There is an energy we create with our thoughts that makes us feel electrified. This energy results from the release of adrenaline. If we don't know what to do with it, it can scare us half to death as it surges through our bodies. It makes us feel nervous, as if we're jumping out of our skins and we can't control it. Remember: we created the energy ourselves. Used properly, this change can be a great source of power.
>
> This energy can empower you, make you more productive, and assist you in doing wonderful things. If we turn the energy inward where it can be of no use, the result is fear and anxiety. The energy turned outward, where it belongs, can empower us. (Bassett, p. 64)

Types of Pressure

There are two broad types of pressure young athletes experience. The first is external (some call it outside motivation) and comes from coaches, fans, parents, and other players. Kids hear words of encouragement from many people. They also pick up on the nonverbal signals and body language from the coaches. External pressure cannot be avoided. The key is found in the way athletes respond to the external pressure forces. Your job is to ensure external pressures are kept positive and reinforcing. Individual players need positive external stimulation. External pressure and motivation can often result in recognition, attention, prizes, and status. Yet these external forces are only effective if the players understand and internalize them into a positive self-image.

The second and more critical form of pressure is internal. This pressure comes from the voice inside us all. We'll call him Mr. Victor. We can't stop him. He never shuts up. He's always talking to us. Behavioral scientists who study this constant internal self-dialogue report that we all have self-talk of over 1000 words per minute. Mr. Victor provides internal beliefs and thoughts that turn into attitudes. These attitudes control our self-image, our performance, and our lives. The great news is we can control him. Lucinda Bassett also writes:

> You are what you think you are, and it's all about your attitude. If you think you aren't happy, you won't be. If you think you can't be successful, you won't be. If you think you're not attractive, you won't be. (Bassett, p. 162)

The trick is to minimize one kind of internal dialogue and maximize another kind. Internal thoughts, words, voices, talking, and dialogue (Mr. Victor) can be negative or positive. We'll call these thoughts and conversations nega-thoughts and posi-thoughts. Nega-thoughts create visions of failure and nonperformance in our minds. Nega-thoughts plant the mental seeds of not being good athletes. On the other hand posi-thoughts plant good images in our own minds. They develop and reinforce the belief that "we can do it" and "we're good at it."

Our Role

It is our responsibility to help every young person develop the ability to maximize positive self-talk. In his book, *Mind Gym*, author Gary Mack writes:

> One key to achieving success in sports is learning how to focus on the task and not let negative thoughts intrude. The mind can concentrate on only one thing at a time. So, rather than suppress what you don't want to happen, you must focus on what you do want to happen. (Mack, p. 9)

As coaches and as parents we can teach our players how to control Mr. Victor. Sometimes it's easy to keep a steady flow of posi-thoughts, especially when a player is on a roll. You've heard it called "being in the zone." Everything seems to be working. This athlete can't miss a ball or a putt, looks great at the net, is making four out of five three-pointers, catches every ball hit or thrown in their direction, etc. Mr. Victor will be positive and supportive. The challenge comes when there is a slump in performance. The athlete hears Mr. Victor not being supportive and positive. The internal voice can be loud. Our job is to help players replace the nega-thoughts with posi-thoughts. First, players must become aware of their inner voice. Then they must use Mr. Victor productively by forcing him to be positive and encouraging. As a result, players who can control Mr. Victor will have improved performance. Shane Murphy writes:

> As you become more aware of your inner voice, you'll come to realize the impact of your thoughts on your behavior. You'll recognize that productive thinking leads to success, while negative thinking usually results in poor, or even di-sastrous, performance. (Murphy, p. 86)

Here are some examples of both kinds of internal dialogue. You'll immediately see how the following statements build up a player and plant good self-images in his or her mind:

▲ "I kick just as well with my secondary foot as with my primary foot."

▲ "I can hit a left-handed pitcher as well as a right."

▲ "My free throw percentage is always high during tournaments."

▲ "I'm good at catching grounders within my range."

▲ "I play my best tennis when I have good racket preparation."

▲ "I love hitting with players on base."

▲ "I love playing football in the mud and rain."

▲ "I do best when I wear my lucky shoes."

▲ "I love hitting the first pitch thrown to me."

▲ "Golfing in the wind is easy for me."

▲ "I love night games under the lights."

▲ "I love playing in close games."

▲ "I always play well at home games."

You get the idea. These mental images and positive self-talk create self-images that are positive and result in higher levels of performance. But on the other side of the coin are many nega-thoughts that act to hinder and hurt an athlete:

▲ "My secondary soccer foot is pathetic."
▲ "I always strike out against left-handed pitchers."
▲ "I never catch baseballs if I have to dive."
▲ "Tennis in bright sunshine is too hard for me to do well."
▲ "I hate the pressure."
▲ "I'd rather strike out not swinging than swinging and look-ing stupid."
▲ "I don't play well in muddy, rainy weather."
▲ "Loud crowds hurt my performance."
▲ "I don't play well in windy conditions."
▲ "The lights hurt my eyes and it's hard to see the balls."
▲ "I can't hit without my batting gloves."
▲ "I can't make a free throw without my lucky ring."
▲ "I never play well against that team."

From his book *The Achievement Zone*, Shane Murphy discusses the power of positive self-talk:

> I cannot overemphasize how important your imagination is in shaping your reality. In a very real way, your imagination helps create the world you live in. You become the person you imagine you are. If you imagine you are successful, you'll be successful. If you imagine you are a failure, you'll probably be a failure.
>
> In order to change the way we act and behave, we must first change the way we look at ourselves. This begins in our minds, in our self-images. (Murphy, p. 69)

It is important for you to understand the critical nature of posi-tive and negative self-talk in your kids, and also in you. You can help your kids develop the ability to increase positive self-talk and positive performance. In this critical area of positive internal self-talk, Karlene Sugarman writes:

Your future is strongly affected by what you believe to be true. Beliefs are built on past experiences along with our perceptions of how things should be. Your beliefs have to be consistent with the results you desire.

As long as you are physically able, your performance will be strongly affected by your own beliefs and confidence in your abilities. This will also determine how much effort you put forth. If you have a strong belief, then no one can sway you. You are the greatest expert of you. All actions are a result of your beliefs and perceptions. (Sugarman, p. 185)

Our bodies and our minds tend to work in unison. They don't conflict with each other. So if our minds believe and visualize negative thoughts, the body will respond accordingly. If people believe they will be successful, they will succeed. The two words "I can't" should not be in anyone's vocabulary. Our job is to promote posi-thoughts in a player's mind. This is accomplished by helping the player convert all forms of pressure into positive internal dialogue.

Here's a little trick that will work wonders. After you explain positive thoughts and negative thoughts to your young athletes, give them each a rubber band to wear on their wrists. They must wear the rubber bands 24 hours per day for a few weeks. Every time they think a nega-thought or say, "I can't," have them snap themselves. They'll be amazed at how often Mr. Victor seems negative. And more importantly they'll learn how to identify nega-thoughts and replace them with posi-thoughts. Shane Murphy also offers these insights:

You must replace negative thinking (which interferes with good performance) with productive thinking (which promotes excellence). Successful people find that when they reduce their negative thoughts, they are more likely to achieve their goals. The best way to eliminate unwanted negative thoughts is to focus on desired productive thoughts. Train your mind to notice negative thoughts and to immediately replace them with productive ones. (Murphy, p. 91)

Nerves

Nerves are feelings we create in our minds. We can help kids understand nerves and then work to control them. Author Les Brown, in his book *It's Not Over Until You Win*, offers this commentary:

> You feel the way you feel because of the thoughts you are thinking. If you are feeling down and out, nearly every thought that comes into your head will be colored by negativity. Often when you have been knocked down by life, you tend to see only the worst in people, in situations, and in your options. You feel hopelessness. Notice that I have not said that your life is hopeless, only that you feel that way. You should not make the mistake of thinking that your feelings reflect the reality. (Brown, p. 147)

Nerves are closely related to the negative inner voice, Mr. Victor. Nerves are the normal queasy feelings of excitement felt inside. Nerves are found on game day, on the way to the facility, during pregame warm-ups, and somewhat during the game. They are found in the anticipation of "How will I do?" and "How will we do?" During intense and active games, the nerves and anticipation subside. The body and mind seem to go into action and take over the situation like the autopilot mechanism on an airplane. But in some sports there is much more time to think, which allows Mr. Victor to become a strong influence. This is when it is critical to control and force posi-thoughts. In *Stress Free Living*, author Trevor Powell discusses how nerves can benefit us if controlled positively:

> We all experience stress, which can affect us in many different ways. A certain level of stress is beneficial and stimulates us to perform well, but too much stress can impair performance. Stress is a positive force that enables you to survive. When you are waiting to cross a busy road you need to be temporarily stressed. Because you are alert, vigilant, and aware of danger, you are more likely to cross safely. Like an electric current, stress increases arousal, gives you energy, and improves your performance. However, if the current is

turned up too high, stress can produce unpleasant effects and cause your performance to deteriorate. Conversely, too little stress can cause you to feel listless and unstimulated, and you are likely to perform slowly and inefficiently. (Powell, p. 6)

Nerves show themselves in two ways. In the negative way, excessive nerves (many people use the term "stress") can cause paralysis. Muscles tighten, palms sweat, and the mind races. Vision, blood flow, and flexibility diminish. The body acts to live out the nega-thoughts. In their positive form, controlled nerves promote the ability to perform at peak levels. The body will live out posi-thoughts. All cylinders are finely tuned. There is just enough positive anxiety to perform well. When we have the more desirable excited nerves, good things happen to our bodies. Blood flow and heart rates rise, adrenaline increases, and breathing and oxygen consumption increase. There are many physical internal positive effects of excited nervousness. This helps explain why so many world records are broken at the Olympics and other major championships. Using nerves to our benefit is a learned skill, and in *The Achievement Zone*, Shane Murphy states:

Recognize that it is very normal to get nervous in competition or when you're being evaluated. Some people will tell you they don't get nervous before a big challenge, but these folks are the exception. If you're like the rest of us and get nervous before a big event, pay attention to your nervousness and welcome it as a good sign. It might seem silly at first, but with practice you will realize that your nervousness really can help you. It can help you concentrate more sharply, it can make you react faster, and it can give you more energy when you need it. (Murphy, p. 132)

Inner Drive

The word "motivation" is an expansion of the word "motive." Motive can be defined as the belief within an individual that drives the person to some form of action. It is an internal attitude that can be taught, learned, and incorporated into a person's thought process. Everyone is self-motivated, either positively or negatively. There is a big difference between winners and losers in sports and in life. Winners are driven by desire. Winning is an internalized attitude and belief system. Motivation and drive become the secrets to our success or failure. Without it, teams play flat. We coaches have all seen our team show up physically to a game but not mentally "up" to play. Their pregame warm-ups are sloppy. They're talking about nongame stuff. They just don't look or sound sharp. We can predict before the game even starts how the team will do.

On the other hand, we've all witnessed our team show up to games with quickness in their warm-ups and all conversation focused on the game to be played. Practice before the game was sharp and the team just looked good. This team was comprised of the same players on the outside but was different on the inside. The positive attitude was contagious and spread to the entire team. On days like this, your team could play another team physically superior to them, but still win. It starts on the inside. The key is found in the internal motivation.

Internal Motivation

Karlene Sugarman offers her thoughts on motivation:

> Motivation is the psychological force that pushes and drives you to work hard—it's the reason that operates as a catalyst to action. Motivation is a state of heart and mind. It's continually seeking out and meeting new challenges, identifying what you love to do and filling your life with that. It's this passion, inner drive and desire that keeps you going each and every day. (Sugarman, p. 90)

There are two primary kinds of internal motivation in place throughout our lives. They are rooted in the emotions of fear and desire. As coaches, we have much influence over these critical attitudes by how we conduct ourselves, our practices, and our games. As parents, we can help players learn to control these powerful emotions. The first kind of internal motivation a player could have is "fear-based." They believe they have to perform in some way or else some negative outcome will occur. The coach will be mad, a parent will be upset, they'll let down the team, they'll look stupid, etc. If an athlete lives by the motto "I have to or else..." the negative nerves show themselves and the mind is subject to many nega-thoughts and negative self-images. Fear-based motivation paralyzes an athlete and he or she will not give 100 percent effort because of the fear of failure. Fear-based motivation focuses on past failures, is very powerful, and creates results contrary to the desired performance we all seek. Fear of failing in some future event is found in a player's head and we (along with Mr. Victor) have a role in keeping the player focused on a better, more positive form of internal motivation. In his book *In the Zone*, Mitchell Perry states it this way:

> When your mind confronts a situation offering just two possible outcomes, one of which has dire consequences, harmful emotions and attitudes emerge, which poison your perspective and diminish your performance. Those emotions include excessive doubt which eventually leads to fear—fear of failure, fear of embarrassment, and all the other fears you have that short-circuit your potential. These are internally created roadblocks to optimum performance. (Perry and Jamison, p. 41)

The second and optimum kind of internal motivation is "desire-based." This motivation is found in the individual player self-dialogue of "I want to..." It is vastly different from "I have to..." The player wants to do some skill or task. They want to look good in future performances based on past successes. They want to do well and perform well. Gary Mack offers the following thoughts:

> People with inner excellence look at competition as a challenge. They are motivated by a desire to succeed rather than by a fear of failure. They possess an unconditional, high self-esteem and self-image. They have a can-do attitude and a will to prepare to win. They believe the harder they work, the harder it is to surrender. They don't quit or play the blame game, and they look after the smallest detail to go the extra mile. Excellence goes beyond winning and losing. (Mack, p. 193)

You can see the difference between the two types of internal thoughts: one way is negative and the other is positive. Desire-based motivation is the ultimate goal our kids can achieve. We as coaches and parents must promote and cultivate a desire-based philosophy. Our job is to replace the fear of failure with a desire for success and high performance by dwelling on the rewards being sought. We must strengthen optimistic desire and enthusiasm to achieve the rewards of success.

Along with all the other avenues presented in this book toward the goal of molding young athletes from the inside out, here is a simple yet powerful technique to foster positive desire-based motivation in every player. In practices and games, coaches should constantly find and reinforce an effort or skill that is done well or a good aspect about every act a player performs. He or she will try 100 percent to continue to improve. Focus on the positive and reward strong effort along with performance. Over time, this approach reduces nega-thoughts and eliminates fear-based motivations. The player keeps trying and succeeds because of desire and persistence. In *Keys to Developing Your Child's Self-Esteem*, Carl Pickhardt writes:

> Human beings are reward-seeking creatures. Most of what they do is motivated by the desire to get what they want. Punishments teach people about what not to do by injuring their well-being. Rewards teach people how to do by encouraging learning. Rewards reinforce self-esteem (feeling good about oneself), whereas punishment reduces self-esteem (feeling bad about oneself). Given the choice, most children prefer treatment that enhances rather than diminishes good feelings about themselves. (Pickhardt, p. 50)

In everything a player does, you can find a positive thing to say. For example, even though the footwork needs improvement while guarding another basketball player, compliment your kid on their quick hands or whatever else they've done well. Tell your tennis player, "Way to hustle to the net," even though they might have missed the return shot and lost the point. Compliment your soccer or football player for making a good sharp pass regardless of some other negative aspect of their performance. Remark how well your infielder does at practices in getting his or her backside down and using two hands (even though the ultimate throw might have been off target).

You get the idea. Find a positive and state it. The player will feel positive and begin to believe in him- or herself. This leads to posi-thoughts and only good results. Now, obviously, the compliments from you must be justified. Also you can't ignore the negative parts of a skill and you can certainly provide good constructive criticism. But you should focus on the positives and constructively work in a positive way on specific areas of a skill requiring improvement. Also offer strong encouragement as an incentive to the player to "keep working on it and improving." This reinforcing technique gradually turns the attitude of the athlete into one of "I want to." Over time the players will develop a desire-based internal motivation. They'll give 100 percent effort and their internal philosophy toward performance will produce positive results. And they'll have more fun participating.

Parents can also have a huge influence by finding positive skills and reinforcing them. When we play with our kids at home or at the park, court, or course, we can build their self-confidence and desire by praising positive performance. As we show our support and approval while playing with our kids, they will adopt positive attitudes. We parents can supplement the work of the coach. It ends up being a joint effort, all aimed at the growth and development of our kids.

Before we close out this chapter on pressure, nerves, and internal motivation, let's put an old adage into the analysis. You've all heard the statement, "Play like you practice." When athletes practice, they have not built up a lot of negative nerves with nega-thoughts and fear-based motivation. They come relaxed with posi-thoughts and a desire-based motivation to learn and have fun. This is a great opportunity for us coaches. With the knowledge of all these internal factors and forces, we can focus on the positive side of each individual and ultimately the entire team. Over time, we guide and control the internal attitudes and belief systems of our players. We truly can help them to play like they practice by removing all the barriers to positive performance as they strive to do their best.

CHAPTER 11

Anger and Frustration

Turning it to good use

Throughout the ages, anger has caused most of the problems found in humanity. Friendships have ended. Parents have divorced. Nations have gone to war. People have damaged each other. Rivers of blood have flowed. Countless hearts have been broken. And the root cause is usually uncontrolled, misdirected anger.

Everyone gets angry. We all get frustrated at some time. It's called human nature. It happens to players, parents, and coaches. Frustration may rear its ugly head in a game situation. It might occur during a practice. It might show up for a lot of reasons. Whatever the cause or situation, it is critical for us to make every attempt to control and learn from our frustration. We adults are in plain view of many players and fans. As role models, the players will know when we're frustrated and they will mimic our behavior, good or bad. Let's examine some root causes of anger and how to deal constructively with this powerful emotion.

Players

There are many reasons players get upset and show anger. Factors that influence how an individual player expresses anger include age, sex, temperament, and family role models. Here are some of the more common reasons we see outbursts of anger.

Acting

Kids can be great actors. Some might be acting upset because they think they're supposed to be mad. Some might act frustrated and be hard on themselves to avoid having others ("us" meaning coaches and parents) be hard on them. Many kids watch a lot of professional sports and witness many exhibitions of misbehavior by so-called "grownups."

For Attention

Kids like to draw attention to themselves. Sometimes if positive game performance doesn't do it, showing frustration does. Attention and recognition, even if negative, can be strong forces. Think back to one of your own young children, or perhaps one you've witnessed, performing a temper tantrum. Those were sure great ways to get attention, weren't they?

Bad Habit

Sometimes habits start early in life. These negative practices become habits and part of our personalities. Our goal is to positively channel and direct anger into new habits of self-control on the outside and the inside.

Appearances

Some kids think that showing frustration in a negative manner looks cool or macho or neat in the eyes of their teammates or other fans. Their behaviors of swearing, throwing things, or other visible outbursts cannot be tolerated by coaches and ultimately lead to negative thinking and nega-thoughts.

Immaturity

This is a reality we must deal with. Many kids (and grownups for that matter) are not in control of their emotions. They're not in mental control of their attitudes or behavior. In the world of psychology and mental therapy, a big area of focus deals with anger management.

Competition

Competition is normal and healthy in childhood. It can energize kids to improve skills and when controlled, it leads to improved self-esteem and performance. There is always a strong competitive drive to be liked by other kids and to be part of the group. This competitive desire can create many positive experiences if expressed productively or it can result in the negative outcomes of fear and anger we sometimes see.

For each of the above reasons that kids display anger, our goal must be to eliminate the underlying motivation. Kids have enough on their minds in youth sports without the added issue of anger and how or when to show it. We can teach kids how to control and use anger to improve their own performance.

Coaches

Coaches often exhibit frustration in plain view of others. As coaches, we must remember there are many eyes on us, more than we know. And our position as a strong role model sends a message to our team of acceptable behavior. Just as with players, there are many reasons coaches display frustration. We'll look at three of the most common.

Immaturity

Face it, many coaches are immature emotionally. But even coaches who normally demonstrate mature behavior can act irrationally at certain times. Mixing immature coaches with young impressionable athletes is a serious situation and can be detrimental to the players and the team. For example, a coach's behavior can be contagious and other players may come to believe the coach's behavior is acceptable. If every athlete under the "guidance" of this coach behaves in a similar way, the entire team will appear negative. Kids won't have fun. Parents won't appreciate the overall team behavior. Other spectators and officials will think badly of the team and its sponsoring organization. And worse yet, bad anger management habits will be formed. As parents, we sometimes have specific complaints about a coach. And sometimes coaches have problems with individual parents. In Chapter 20 we'll cover effective ways to deal with grievances you might encounter.

Acting

Many coaches resort to a physical display of frustration in order to make a point to the team. They may be upset only on the outside and trying to communicate their seriousness to the rest of the team.

True Frustration

Sometimes coaches have a bad day at work. Experiencing bad team behavior or poor performance can snap their patience. Obviously we want to minimize or eliminate this from happening altogether, but when it does, maintaining proper self-control becomes important.

Handling Anger and Frustration

These emotions usually result from a perception by the player (or coach) of a failure. The failure can be a physical mistake or a mental mistake. Everyone on the team must recognize that failure is part of the game. Managing this failure is the key to how we perform and how we continue throughout the balance of the game. Completely ignoring our failures is not the correct response. We must help our players accept the fact they will make mistakes, that it is natural and temporarily acceptable to get frustrated, as long as they get only mad enough to identify and learn from their mistake in a short-term constructive way. Then, it's time to proceed without dwelling on the original mistake in a negative way.

Another cause of anger stems from a feeling of helplessness or a lack of power. In this case, the anger goes away as helplessness goes away. We can help avoid and eliminate much of this type of anger by solid preparation and physical advancement. This will minimize feelings of powerlessness. Here's another way to help your young athlete (and even yourself) during times of anger or frustration. Have the player talk to him- or herself (with self-talk) in the same way he or she would talk to a friend or teammate dealing with frustration. We are harder on ourselves than we'd ever be on a friend and this isn't fair to us or our performance.

You'll remember that we covered internal dialogue and the voice of Mr. Victor. He can benefit us greatly with posi-thoughts. We must teach our players to control Mr. Victor and rechannel any negative feelings into positively focused attitudes. Again, we must teach and preach that every player (and coach) will make mistakes and this is okay as long as we learn from them and grow because of them. Mistakes should be viewed as opportunities for improvement. Failure becomes a vehicle for future success. True success never comes easily. In his book *Working Out, Working Within*, author Jerry Lynch offers the following comments on success and failure:

> Sports and exercise give us plenty of opportunity to become internally at peace with failure and loss. Everyone experiences setbacks; they cannot be avoided. It is said there are two kinds of performers in the world: Those who fail and those who will. Acceptance of this fact will help you to be more accepting of your shortcomings, not only in sports, but in all of life. Great athletes and performers become winners because they seem to have a very high tolerance for failure. (Lynch and Huang, p. 180)

Every successful person, from any field of achievement, will tell you there were many failures along the way. The road to success is always paved with bricks of gain and bricks of loss. Great parents will tell you they've made mistakes. Great business people will admit their failures. The best professional athletes have stories of failure in their lives. Failure is common to everyone. The key to success is learning from our failures and avoiding repeating them without getting frustrated. Karlene Sugarman addresses the topic of learning from failure as follows:

> Problems are really opportunities to achieve something even greater. Failure and success are equal opportunities for learning. When you fail to learn, you have learned to fail. When Thomas Edison was attempting to make the lightbulb, he failed many times. Although in his eyes, he didn't fail, he just discovered another way not to do it!

> High self-confidence gets you moving toward success instead of trying to avoid failure. If you do fail, which you will do from time to time, don't hang on to those failures. To be successful you need to deal with and master failure. Evaluate your performance not yourself, your acts are measurable, you, as a total human being, are not. You will still be a valuable person regardless of your sporting results. This is a very basic fact, but one many people seem to forget. (Sugarman, p. 184)

Here are a few final points to help you and your athletes control exhibitions of frustration on the outside and their harmful effects to our insides. Players need to remember there are two halves to the game, offense and defense. If and when they make a mistake in one half of the game, they have to realize the team still needs them. They cannot let down or give up. Excessive uncontrolled nega-thoughts can paralyze a player to the point of having low performance for the balance of the game. The player should take responsibility for the mistake and then commit to avoiding future repetitions by hard work and improvement. He or she must realize they have a contribution to make and a responsibility to the rest of the team. In addition, players and coaches need to be reminded they are representing their school, community, or organization. They also represent themselves to all fans and friends. Showing frustration in negative ways reflects badly on the organization and the individual.

Obviously it's easy to list causes of frustration in players and coaches. It's easy to say we coaches should control our players and ourselves on the inside and the outside. But this is difficult to do sometimes. After all, we are human. This topic is important and we as coaches need to be aware of its potentially positive or negative results. We can begin by improving how we handle frustration and if we fail and behave in a manner beneath our own expectations, we must be big enough to apologize, especially to our team. This will show we make mistakes (like any player) and will learn from them. Controlling frustration becomes another lesson we can teach in the life of an athlete.

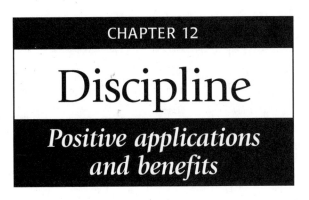

CHAPTER 12

Discipline

Positive applications and benefits

Put on your coach's hat. We're going to examine the sensitive topic of discipline. This is often a controversial area that all coaches must deal with. There are different ways to administer various types of discipline. As we discuss it, discipline need not be negative if pre-communicated and presented in the proper way. It is important to use discipline as a positive learning tool for the betterment of the individual player and the team. We've all heard the term "tough love." This philosophy accurately describes how we should approach discipline. Administering discipline is the "necessary evil" part of a coach's responsibility, and is nothing to be afraid of. When the entire area of discipline is handled properly, coaches encourage team unity and gain player respect.

The Philosophy of Discipline

Discipline is a reaction to specific behaviors. Effective discipline is dependent on the causes of the original behavior. Before any discipline is administered, it is a coach's critical responsibility to ensure that the chosen tactic of discipline is the appropriate response. Simply put, there are two categories of behavior that are seen in young actions and attitudes.

The first type of negative behavior stems from willfully ignoring and breaking the rules. The young person purposely intends to act in a certain way. The second general type of behavior is a product of common youthful immaturity and irresponsibility. In this second case, there is not an intent to ignore or break the rules.

You will see that both areas are different and require different reactions. The first intentional category requires some form of discipline. The second requires a heaping portion of patience and understanding. But irresponsibility without the intent to break the rules is not grounds for discipline. The balance of this chapter will focus on how to effectively deal with discipline as it pertains to the intentional violation of the rules.

Rules

For discipline to be understood and accepted by everyone involved there have to be clearly defined standards of behavior. It is a good idea for all coaches to discuss and develop a set of common ground rules and regulations early in the practice portion of the season. General areas to cover include attire, timeliness, acceptable behavior, language, fighting, and treatment of others. You can probably think of many more topics. The goal is to have all coaches and team members on the same page. This consistent approach is no different than having both parents in a family agree on a set of rules and standards for their children, plus the consequences if those standards are violated.

Administering Individual Discipline

There are two options to consider when discipline is required of a player. A coach must determine how to discipline an athlete to achieve long-term goals. The first technique is one-on-one. This involves just the coach and the person. The coach can use this opportunity to offer constructive criticism by stating the unacceptable act or situation. He or she can also explain how discipline will be administered and state future consequences if there is a repeat of the problem.

For you coaches, one-on-one discipline is probably the safest and most effective. Here's how to discuss an issue with a child. First and foremost, make sure the child understands that you, as the coach, are not attacking the individual child. Make it clear that the child has violated a known rule and for the good of the entire team, you are being forced to address the problem. Explain why the rules are important and restate any specifics relevant to the situation. Then calmly state the consequence of the discipline and carry out the discipline. A strong message will be sent to all team members when a coach administers consistent and fair discipline.

The second method of discipline for an individual is to use him or her as an example. This involves making a point in front of the whole team for the good of the team. If you use an individual as a vehicle for a bigger lesson, be sure to lighten up a little and not be too harsh. Simply state the infraction and future expectations. This tactic requires skill and good judgment on your part to use the right athlete for the right lesson at the right time. If you as a coach are not 100 percent sure you can pull off this touchy maneuver, don't even try it. The risk of serious negative impact to a single child is too great. The young person could suffer short-term humiliation because of you. He or she could also be the victim of negative behaviors from other team members because of the specific discipline consequences you select. Be careful.

The key to both forms of disciplining a single player is to make sure you criticize the behavior and not attack the player personally. There will be times and situations you will administer discipline one-on-one. There will be other times when it will be appropriate to use the experience of one player as a model for the whole team. Look at it this way: When a player makes a great play in a clutch situation, we as coaches use that performance as a positive example to motivate others. In the same way, we can positively use discipline to help all players. Your attitude and demeanor of rational calmness will be as important as the lesson learned from the actual act itself. Don't ever underestimate the nonverbal message of your tone or your sincerity. The kids will know where your heart is.

Administering Team Discipline

On rare occasions you may find it appropriate or necessary to discipline the entire team if the whole team has knowingly broken a rule. If this situation arises you must clarify the infraction and refer to the preseason expectations that were communicated to all players and parents (more on this topic later). As a team they win and lose together. If discipline is appropriate, the entire team is included. As a coach you must make any discipline fit the crime and not go overboard. Use good judgment in this area. Discipline is a part of life. If a person violates the rules, positive lessons can be learned.

The question arises whether coaches should discipline an entire team for the bad behavior of a few team members. Some coaches do this to make a point. Most coaches believe it is an unfair way to use the tool of discipline. Kids who have not broken any rules cannot usually control the conduct of other team players. So it's unfair of us coaches to dole out uniform discipline to all based on the behavior of a few. It is better to address the individual violators and act with them accordingly.

Precommunication

Communicating team rules and expectations is a critical part of any sport. It's important that every player understand the boundaries of behavior and any negative ramifications. Coaches must communicate to parents also. They need to understand all team guidelines. Good coaches will state the rules early and have them written for distribution so there are no surprises. In Chapter 20 we'll cover group meetings between parents and coaches. We'll examine effective ways to communicate the rules, expectations, and standards.

Fairness and Consistency

In today's world of excessive permissiveness and the fact that many kids never hear the word "no," young athletes often lack proper discipline at home and at school. As a coach trying to enforce a rule, you might hit resistance from a player or a parent. Again, pre-communication gives you the basis from which to carry through on your disciplinary act. When you as a coach follow your own pre-communicated rules, you avoid treating different players in different manners, which otherwise could lead to the charge of being inconsistent. Players may not like having gotten caught or being disciplined but if it is communicated properly, they won't be surprised. If discipline is used only when necessary and administered as laid out in this section, you will earn a certain amount of esteem. Also players will respect the fact you were forced into a situation requiring discipline for the good of the individuals and team.

It is important for parents to understand and trust the motives of a coach in this sensitive area of discipline. If you as a parent have a child on the receiving end of discipline, you should attempt to gain all the facts before taking any sides. Learn as much as possible to determine if the discipline is appropriate. If the coach is being fair and consistent, for the good of your young person (and the team) you must support the coach. As much as we parents often want to shelter our kids from any kind of discipline, this chapter has shown it can be a useful tool for growth and success.

As adults, our goal is to instill positive, desire-based motivation. If we administer discipline incorrectly or inappropriately, we hurt individual and team growth. But if we use the tool of discipline properly, everybody can prosper and grow in the classroom we call youth sports.

Chapter Highlights
to Improve Your Game Plan

▲ Pressure can be desirable if channeled and controlled.

▲ We can teach our young athletes to positively control their internal self-talk (Mr. Victor).

▲ Positive mental images can be translated into positive performance.

▲ Motivation can be rooted in the positive emotions of desire or the negative emotions of fear.

▲ We can help kids control their natural anger and frustration.

▲ Players and coaches display negative behavior for a variety of reasons.

▲ Failure is natural and we must help our kids understand, anticipate, and deal constructively with mistakes and failures.

▲ Discipline is a positive tool we can use to develop kids.

▲ When rules are intentionally broken, positive discipline can benefit each player and the team.

CHAPTER 13

Progress and Success

Very important yet often ignored

What is success? How do we measure progress throughout the pregame season and game season? We must examine the important "-ess" words of progress and success. To some, this seems like a difficult part of the game to address and quantify. But let's look at how we can measure the "-ess" words. Kids will love to help set goals of success and monitor how they are doing individually and as a team. This chapter will deal with different forms and types of success from the perspectives of the player, the team, and finally the coach. You'll want your coach's hat on. And as parents, you also have the opportunity to understand and implement how you can help your kids grow.

Definitions

Author Mike Krzyzewski deals with the issue of true success in the following words:

> If you're always striving to achieve a success that is defined by someone else, I think you'll always be frustrated. There will never be enough championships. There will never be

enough wins. And when you finally attain them, if you're lucky enough to do so, they'll only be numbers. Somebody will say you were great or that you were successful, but ultimately you'll know it's an empty success.

The only way to get around such an unhappy ending is to continually define your own success. And it begins in the preseason before everything bursts into full bloom. Your definition of success should have more depth than the equivalent of winning a national championship. It should be whatever passion moves you deep in your heart. My passion is to coach and do things to the best of my ability. I want our team to get better every day. If we can do that, the other stuff will take care of itself. (Krzyzewski, p. 54)

The definition of success varies with each player because of individual standards, desires, and perceived athletic abilities. Internal success comes from the realization of individual and team accomplishments. Players judge success in short-term timeframes. Our job is to help players develop an attitude of observing success with a "big picture" view of the entire season. We need to look at the season as one entity from beginning to end and judge overall progress and success from that standpoint. To determine and monitor progress, coaches should conduct one-on-one conversations with each player early in the practice season. This is the time to ask various questions to identify several personality traits and attitudes. Regarding success, each athlete should be asked for their favorite and least favorite:

▲ Parts of the game
▲ Positions played
▲ Practice drills, etc.

When coaches ask "why?" to each of the answers, this is a golden chance to gain great insight into each player. The results of these conversations should be kept for use throughout the season. Mike Krzyzewski also writes:

> Mutual commitment helps overcome the fear of failure—especially when people are part of a team sharing and achieving goals. It also sets the stage for open dialogue and honest conversation. Early in the preseason, I'll often have a casual conversation with one of our players about his personal life. And because we already have that commitment to each other, it's easy for us to talk. He already knows that I'm on his side and that I'll always be there for him.
> (Krzyzewski, p. 15)

The definitions of team success and progress will be tied into individual definitions but on a larger big-picture scale. Success cannot be judged solely on wins and losses. These statistics are important for rank standings and post-season play but are not the single driving factors. Other aspects of success must include an analysis of how the team has done in other areas. Coaches should monitor and communicate the development of:

▲ Improved levels of play and performance
▲ Increased levels of intensity
▲ Playing strong heads-up ball, etc.

The team definition of success should focus on these external and internal attitudinal areas. As coaches, we should continually keep track of the overall improvement of the team throughout the season as a measurement of progress. To help in this ongoing process of monitoring and evaluating a team's improvement, we need to begin with defined goals. Karlene Sugarman offers her thoughts on goals and coach/player relationships in the following:

> To get the most out of each player and make the team experience a positive one, you must understand the individuality of your players and the dynamics of group interaction. Knowing the patterns in the evolvement of a group will give you a valuable perspective. It's essential to know the needs, strengths and weaknesses of your athletes. Great leaders must see into the hearts and heads of their players. They must know what makes each of them tick and how

they are motivated. It's hard to be responsive to their needs if you are unsure of what they are! That's why it is imperative to know the mental make-up of your athletes. (Sugarman, p. 74)

Goals

Common sense says that if you don't know where you're going, you won't get there. You've all heard the saying, "If you fail to plan, you are planning to fail." These simple yet true thoughts state the importance of setting and striving for individual and team goals. Winners do not wander around aimlessly through a season or life. The very word "aim-less-ly" says it all. Obviously we cannot hit a target if we don't know what the target is. On the topic of goals, author Gary Mack writes:

Goal setting is a master skill for personal growth and peak performance. I can't stress this too much. Without goals, where will you go in life? If you don't know where you are headed, you're probably going to wind up somewhere other than where you want to be.

Goal setting is a way of bringing the future into the present so you can take action now. Goals improve performance. Goals improve the quality of practices. They clarify expectations and help increase self-confidence by seeing yourself get better. (Mack, p. 60)

It is our job to identify and organize all goals whether they are individual or team goals. We should allow the team members to set various smaller goals that have high probabilities of being attained. Goals should be set just out of reach to promote hard work and feelings of achievement as the goals are met. These goals can be set in the one-on-one conversations with the coach, and they can also be established in a team discussion setting. For the individual player goals, ask them during the one-on-one meetings what they want out of the season. Ask them for their specific personal goals. Some goals will be physical; some will be internal or attitudinal. Physical goals could include specific skill improvements or individual performance goals. Attitudinal goals could include the desire to have fun, to learn, to make friends, or simply to enjoy a particular sport. Write down each player's short-term and long-term goals. Some will be honest while some will say what they think we want to hear. Either way, you'll learn a lot about each player.

Larger goals should also be formulated. Have the team set some short-term attainable goals. You should also get the team to set a few bigger goals even if they have a lower probability of being achieved. In the team discussion, try to get input from all players so they "buy into" the team goals. Just like the individual target goals, team goals must be exact and identifiable. As you set individual or team goals, keep in mind the same philosophy we covered in the topic of "winning at all costs" versus "striving to win." "Win at all costs" is result-oriented and result-focused. "Striving to win" is action-oriented and performance-oriented. Athletes and teams with "action focus" goals that they have set by themselves will play and perform better. So as you set goals, make sure they are focused on actions and performance and not on a result (like the number of wins or losses). Result goals focus on competing with others and involve many external factors that cannot be controlled. Action/performance goals are those in which a player or the team competes with itself. These goals are more controllable and ultimately more rewarding.

Perfectionism

A damaging unrealistic "result focus" requires perfection and this trait is negative. People don't want to be around a person driven to be perfect. People would rather be with someone who's imperfect. Remember that it's okay to be imperfect. The drive for perfection often creates a fear of failing, which paralyzes the player so they won't try anything new. We can help avoid perfectionism and teach our young athletes to replace perfection (which is based on an outcome) with the philosophy of striving for excellence. As we work with our kids to guide them to do their best, they can focus their attention inward toward happiness, perseverance, dedication, and fun. In her book *From Panic to Power*, Lucinda Bassett puts it this way:

> One of the most wonderful gifts I can offer my children is to help them believe that they don't have to be perfect. As a matter of fact, although I have taught them to have high standards, I have also taught them not to strive for perfection because it doesn't exist. It's similar to the misconception that things should always be fair. Nothing and no one is perfect. So, if there's no such thing as perfection, how do we know we've done our best? That's easy. When we can say to ourselves, "I feel good about what I just did," or "I'm proud of that," or "I feel good about myself for making that effort." How about, "It didn't work out but I gave it a heck of a try." When we can say any of these things, then we've accomplished something! (Bassett, p. 63)

How do we monitor our goals? After all goals have been established, we must track individual and team progress. We also must continually communicate with all players the growth or lack thereof as it pertains to the pre-set goals. These action-oriented goals can range from a single individual's desire to go three for three (hits, free throws, pass receptions, shots on goal, etc.) or a team's goal of playing solid physical and mental ball in a three-game tournament in a rival community. Ongoing mid-season reviews are an excellent vehicle to provide valuable feedback from the coaches to the team and vice versa. Ask the players how we as a team are doing and identify pluses and minuses. List potential adjustments for improvement and provide appropriate reinforcements.

You can communicate the status of the team with the players. State the successes and the goals that have been met. Also mention the temporary shortfalls or unaccomplished goals and help the team develop strategies to meet those goals. Emphasize to the team its responsibility to help achieve its original goals set earlier in the practice season. Tell the team that the coaches cannot physically achieve the team goal, only the players can do that. We'll discuss the area of "responsibility" more in Chapter 16, which deals with the teaching of values.

At the end of your season, you have another opportunity to review the team goals in a more public setting. This is the time to be positive. Every team appreciates a season-ending grand finale. Team picnics are great fun for this one last event. As coach you can restate for all to hear some individual player goals (without embarrassing any individual) and explain how a goal was met. End on a high supportive note. Maybe you could have a gathering at your home or another parent's home. Or you might consider a parent/child game at the local field, diamond, or court with refreshments. Another good time for this special season-ending activity is right after the last game. You could get all appropriate gear and uniforms returned. These events can be a great way to recap and conclude a wonderful team-season experience.

The previous chapters can be summed up in a catchy phrase: Conceive, believe, achieve. When players develop and communicate goals, they *conceive* the strategic plan for the season. As the players develop positive internal levels of self-confidence, they *believe* in themselves and their team. And finally, young athletes *achieve* success as they perform and grow throughout the entire season. "Conceive, believe, achieve" is short and sweet but says it all.

Chapter Highlights
to Improve Your Game Plan

▲ It's important to set individual and team goals.

▲ Progress and success must be periodically monitored to help every child improve.

▲ Perfectionism is a bad trait and we can help to eliminate it.

SECTION IV

You, The Coach

Notes and Thoughts

CHAPTER 14

The Hats We Wear

Coaches have a hundred jobs

There was a time when we coaches just brought a ball to practice and showed the players what to do with it. All we did was coach the mechanical physical aspects of the game. Today we have multiple roles and responsibilities. Like it or not we will all play a large role in the short- and long-term lives of the kids on our teams. This is nothing to be shied away from. We should embrace the opportunity to be a positive influence on the young people in our care.

As parents, it is important that we understand the many roles and responsibilities of a coach. Coaches make powerful impressions on our kids. They are influential to the physical and psychological growth of our young people. We must understand their world so that we can help them mold our kids from the inside out.

Influences

The definition of coach is: (1) a guide, a leader, a person dedicated to individual player and team development, (2) to act as a guide, to instill and reinforce skills and values to be applied in games and in life, and (3) being many things to many people.

We all have a greater influence on kids than they realize. They don't know it at the time but later in life they'll remember values and attitudes we taught them. We help kids develop physically, mentally, and emotionally.

Primary Adult Figure

The traditional two-parent family has undergone drastic changes in recent years. There are more broken families and mixed families than before. Today's young people are subjected to many societal problems and suffer the consequences. Fortunately (or unfortunately depending on how you look at it) we play a bigger role in a child's world than coaches of yesteryear did. Bettie Youngs provides some numbers and food for thought:

> The "family" has changed. Of the more than ninety-eight million American households, almost twenty-three million consist of one adult and one child. Today, nearly 74 percent of women are in the workforce, and many of these are the head of their household. According the 1990 census, of every one hundred children born today:
>
> • seventeen will be born out of wedlock;
>
> • forty-eight will have parents who divorce before the children are eighteen;
>
> • sixteen will have parents who separate;
>
> • six will have at least one parent die before the children are eighteen.
>
> That means that of every one hundred children, only thirteen will become adults in "normal" families. (Youngs, p. 174)

Role Model (Positive or Negative)

In society today, there are many strange people who should not be around young people. Today's kids are more susceptible to influences than before and it is critical that we as coaches demonstrate exemplary societal behavior. We read about it in our newspapers. Every time there is an incident involving one bad apple,

THE HATS WE WEAR

it reflects badly on us all. When parents learn about horrible coaching behavior in their own community, or somewhere else in the United States, they rightfully become concerned. Parents expect and deserve coaches who exhibit proper behavior. Parents will want assurance that their kids are in the care of qualified coaches.

In the world of professional sports there is much idiotic behavior. While it makes the headlines, too often it seems to be excused. There are many negative role models to whom our kids look up. People believe that involvement in sporting activities will build character. But then we hear about many professional athletes with little character. We can counter their bad influences by living out more positive behaviors and discussing the negative actions of some of those multimillion dollar athletes.

Counselor/Educator

We often find ourselves dealing with nonsports issues of academic performance, drugs, alcohol, and other counterproductive activities. Early teens are exposed to a lot of potentially bad influences. Bettie Youngs also writes:

> More and more children are showing signs of increasing stress, strains, and pressures too obvious to dismiss. Today, the toll of stress on children may be even greater then we suspect.
>
> • More than one in three children suffer stress-related illness, including dizziness, chest pains, wheezing, stomach problems, and headaches.
>
> • There are nearly 2,000 teenage suicides a year.
>
> • Fifteen percent of high school students are considered problem drinkers.
>
> • One-third of all American schoolchildren under the age of 18 use illegal drugs.
>
> • One-third of all violent crimes in America are committed by people under 20 years old.
>
> • Students carry an estimated 270,000 guns to school daily.

• The school dropout rate continues to soar each year (it is now over 40 percent).

• Each year one out of every ten teenage girls between 13 and 17 becomes pregnant (more than one million). (Youngs, p. 6)

There are unfortunately many more alarming figures. Kids today believe they are growing up in a society that is hostile and indifferent toward them. With the proliferation of our news media age, today's kids have lost the stage of childhood innocence. They also are taught a wide array of crisis topics about environmental disasters, worldwide disease, epidemic catastrophes, economic collapse, and a host of others. As they combine fear with disillusion and childhood uncertainty, they often look for ways to escape. Common outlets are gangs, violence, crime, delinquency, sexual activity, smoking, and drug use. These are powerful temptations to many of our kids. There are ad campaigns against smoking and drugs but as coaches we need to address reasons why kids should not participate in these harmful temptations. Also we should explain the negative effects of steroids at an early age. Today's young kids have a greater attitude of acceptance toward steroids than most of us would assume. Many of us will have to address one or more of these areas directly. It's part of our job and we can be a positive influence.

Coaches have unique roles in the lives of young athletes. We can send strong messages about the harmful effects of drug and alcohol use. You should talk about these issues early in the practice season team meetings (to parents also). In your serious team discussions, explain that the drugs of alcohol, tobacco, as well as all other illegal drugs are harmful. Convey to each player that he or she is important to the team's success and they'll play better if they stay drug free. Offer your open ear if a player knows of a person or has a problem of their own needing professional help.

The National Alliance for Youth Sports has clear standards relating to drug and alcohol issues. The information below focuses on the negative effects of drug and alcohol use. Phrases and excerpts come from the coach's handbook, pages 18 to 19. Here are some questions and answers you should present to your team.

What are drugs?

Drugs are chemicals that change the way our bodies and minds work. Alcohol is a drug that slows down reaction time, coordination and judgment. Tobacco can cause shortness of breath, increased heart rate and reduces the ability to exercise.

How do other drugs affect performance?

Every drug affects us differently. Many cause muscles, brain and lungs to operate incorrectly. Some cause the body and heart to work harder than is normal. Others slow the reflexes and coordination. Marijuana harms the way a body concentrates and moves. Cocaine and crack negatively affect heart rate, blood pressure and attention span.

What are anabolic steroids?

Some athletes take these drugs because they believe the drugs will make them stronger and faster. There are many short- and long-term negative side effects from steroids. One is a prolonged recovery time to heal from injuries and infections. Other effects include stunted growth in height, increased risk of joint damage and increased aggressiveness with violent actions.

Do drugs hurt other players on the team?

Yes. When some players engage in tobacco, alcohol and other illegal drugs, they impact the entire team.

Drugs and alcohol are serious issues and we must be positive role models. Kids are exposed to these dangers at younger and younger ages. We cannot ignore the topic and can make ourselves available to listen. We can also watch for the signs of drug or alcohol use of erratic performance, mood swings, secrecy, and major lifestyle and dress changes. If as coaches you become aware of drug use, you should address the problem by getting help for the young person through their family or local public agency. When we help a young person deal with the problem of drug or alcohol use, we improve their life and maybe save it.

When the topic turns to academics, it is important for coaches to emphasize that every athlete should strive to do his or her best in school. If players are motivated to do well in academics they will have a similar internal discipline and motivation in sports. A solid education is the key to future success. And don't let them think they'll be a professional athlete someday and can ignore education. We all know the tiny percentage of youth athletes who even come close to the big leagues.

Disciplinarian (Tough Love)

We've covered the how-to's of discipline in Chapter 12. The general topic is included here just to illustrate one of our many roles. Discipline is a tool we have at our disposal to help players on our teams understand the importance of rules and behavioral boundaries.

Doctor

One of our primary obligations to our players (and their families) is the physical well-being of each athlete. It's always a good idea to observe the playing facilities prior to any practices or games and look for obvious potential hazards. It's another good idea to be aware of a parent with a cell phone in case of an emergency or if any parent has medical training. You never know when these things might be needed.

As coach, you should know basic first-aid techniques and be able to calmly control any medical situation. You'll likely be exposed to cuts, bruises, dehydration or heat cramps, heat exhaustion, strains, and sprains. Less common injuries include dislocations and fractures. Your main responsibility with most of these situations is to keep the player/patient calm and treat any potential injury as a serious injury. Use good judgment with first-aid situations and don't be afraid to ask for help from other knowledgeable parents or coaches.

Self-Protection

In today's world people get sued at the drop of a hat. Since we put ourselves in the visible fishbowl of working closely with a lot of kids, the effects of excessive unnecessary litigation carry over into youth sports. We need to be aware of this constant possibility and guard against any problems. Charges against coaches could stem from our mental and verbal behavior with the players. The primary way to avoid untrue claims is to make sure there are clearly communicated rules of behavior. Also, we must remember to use constructive criticism and critique a player's behavior only.

Regarding the physical side of potential lawsuits, we are protected if we incorporate a general personal rule of never touching a player's body. Handshakes and high-fives are appropriate but anything else could be viewed negatively. All it takes is a charge of harassment by a parent whose kid is not starting or gets cut and your coaching days could be over. The solution is to protect yourself as much as possible from any perception of harassment.

Remember in our chapter on goal setting and success, you were encouraged to have one-on-one conversations with your players to establish goals and develop a perception about their level of motivation. These one-on-one meetings cannot be in an isolated area. You need to conduct those in plain view of others. Never be alone with a player, period! And to avoid collusion by several players, you should incorporate the philosophy of dual leadership presence. This way there will be at least two grownups at any event (you and another coach).

Another area of necessary self-protection involves liability and insurance. Today most organizations, communities, and schools have insurance for their coaches. We've all heard horror stories about coaches getting sued and losing their homes because of an accident that occurred after instructing an athlete to do something. You must check with your organization to identify what insurance exists and make sure you are covered.

We do not want to end this chapter on a sour note, but these are considerations we all must be aware of. It's just something we as responsible, thorough coaches have to do. As this chapter illustrates, we wear many hats as a coach of young people and therein lies some of our greatest challenges and rewards.

Chapter Highlights
to Improve Your Game Plan

▲ Coaches have a tremendous impact on kids.

▲ Many kids are subjected to destructive family environments and societal influences.

▲ Coaches can discuss the serious issues of tobacco, drug and alcohol use, and their negative effects.

▲ Never be alone with a young athlete and always have another adult (two-deep leadership) present at youth sports activities.

▲ Make sure you have insurance and liability protection if you are a coach.

CHAPTER 15

Teaching Mechanics

Fun physical skills become subconscious actions

Walk into any bookstore and look through the sports section. You'll see various instructional books and tapes on the physical aspects of an individual youth sport. There is no shortage of technical resources to help coaches learn the physical mechanics of their specific sport. For our purposes, we will not go into the individual details of practice drill techniques or skill development for specific youth sports. Our goal is to mold every young person across the broad spectrum of all youth sports.

As an illustration of how to conduct a typical practice that can be tailored any sport, this chapter ends with a sample detailed practice session. But first let's examine the mental side of proper well-done practices and physical preparation. Some of our most important tasks are to instill a sense of individual cooperation and team unity, assess the individual levels of each player and the team as a whole, and finally to select ways to improve the players' skill. Our job of teaching the physical basics of any sport is important. We'll look at some "hows and whys" of running positive practices. Our goal should be to create and run exciting, involved, fast-paced practices. After all, the traditional definition of "practice" is drill, routine, drill, hard work, drill, and more drill. Author Karlene Sugarman writes about hard work and practice:

> So many times you see athletes only practicing the things that they are already proficient at. The committed athlete knows that he has to push hard when it comes to the things that are difficult for him and turn those weaknesses into strengths. Nobody hands you excellence on a silver platter. You earn it through preparing and persisting in the face of all obstacles. Obstacles are new challenges, not walls to stop you. You need to understand that your commitment to your mental game will pay off big, if it is something you work hard at every day, just like your physical skills. You must persist through the discomfort of adding something new to your training, and realize that it can help you reach the goals you have set for yourself. Quality physical practice and mental practice, combined, lead to better performances. (Sugarman, p. 27)

The Basics

Learning and practicing the basic skills of any sporting technique can be boring in the eyes of kids. Face it, practices can be mundane, and this creates potential distractions in the young athletes. Their motivation and desire decrease. When they are bored their minds have time to wander and they'll often ask themselves or others why they have to do a certain drill. They might be genuinely curious. This is a good chance for you to explain the drill being questioned and its benefits. Mike Krzyzewski gives us his philosophy:

> How much I speak to the players on our team is important, but they'll forget a lot of what they hear. It's also important to make sure they watch and observe through action and videotape. Usually, the team will remember more of what they see. But the most critical aspect of our team training is what the guys actually do and what they understand.

110

So we perform all kinds of game-like drills over and over again. Such repetition is designed to refine physical habits. And it is key to ensuring that a team will perform well in a real-life situation—because the group will not only hear and see what we tell them, they'll actually execute what we tell them. (Krzyzewski, p. 88)

Our job is to teach basic skills in a way that the players develop proficiency. Because our bodies perform best to well-learned skills, the key is physical repetition. You've heard it called muscle memory. It begins on the inside and works its way out. It begins as mental effort with mental focus on our body and eventually our body takes over. It is the state when a player has done a skill so many times he or she no longer has to think about it. Performing the skill goes from being a conscious effort at the beginning to being transferred to the subconscious level.

Once a skill advances to the subconscious level the player is free to use his or her mind on the mental aspects of the game. We do not want the mind to be involved in the physical acts of performance during game situations. This can only be accomplished through proper (or incorrect if you teach incorrect skills) repetitions over and over again. At first with any new skill or skill modification, the mind must be involved. Your constant reinforcement becomes critical at this point so the correct skill becomes subconscious.

At the beginning it is demanding and frustrating for any player to mentally learn and perform a new physical skill. Project yourself back in time to the first time you tried a new skill. You undoubtedly focused hard mentally and consciously. You were determined to make your body do what your mind wanted it to do. There are many examples you could think of. Let's take the task of learning to ride a bike. At first, you gritted your teeth and tried with every muscle in your body to keep that bike upright. It seemed impossible. Then, miraculously, after you got the hang of balance and muscular control, that activity became simple. It turned into muscle memory. It became like second nature to you. As skill mechanics become muscle memory and automatic, the mind can focus on what it can and should control. The mind can act as the facilitator of the body. The voice inside, "Mr. Victor," becomes free to help us in positive ways. Some things the mind should control are game situations, strategies, what to do in case (you fill in the blank), being aware of field conditions, adjusting to umpires and referees, paying attention to coach instructions, and controlling Mr. Victor.

Muscle memory is the goal. It builds critical confidence and allows the athlete to "let" their body perform. They no longer have to consciously "force" or "make" their body function. The most successful athletes "let it happen" and don't try to exert mental control over a muscle memory (subconscious) act. The term "choking" is the exact result of someone not trusting his or her own muscle memory and trying to think too much about his or her physical performance. In this case the player perceives too much stress and nega-thoughts. This conflicts with muscle memory performance and destroys reaction time, responsiveness, and alertness. The result is panic and choking. It's all avoidable if we help young players learn to "let it happen." Karlene Sugarman provides some insight to the phenomenon of choking:

> Choking starts out as a cognitive problem and ends up a physical one, and this negatively affects performance. Choking begins with negative self-talk and fear. It is the interpretation of a task as threatening, or a situation as extremely important, which causes feelings of tension and anxiety, both of which distract you from the task at hand and therefore impede performance. The key word is interpretation, because in actuality, the situation isn't making you tense, you are making yourself tense. Believe it or not, anxiety doesn't exist outside of your own head. You start questioning your ability to get a hit, complete a pass, throw a strike, make a play, etc. All these negative thoughts begin snowballing and pretty soon you're thinking about consequences—just a whirlwind of thoughts that can't seem to be stopped. (Sugarman, p. 190)

Here's a simple example of how your mind can get in the way of performance. Pretend there is a board that measures 10 inches wide by 10 feet long lying on the floor of your home. If you were asked to walk the distance of the board while it was lying on the floor, it would be easy. But if the board gets suspended between two buildings 200 feet in the air, the simple task would get difficult. Yet the board is the same board with the same dimensions. The only thing that has changed is how you now perceive the "simple" task. Your mind has just created a bunch of new conditions and factors. As a result, your performance would suffer.

Confidence

Have you ever wondered why an individual sporting program or community can get hundreds of young kids to start a sport and by the time this same group gets to high school, only a handful are still involved? Why do we lose so many potentially good athletes? There are many reasons, such as other sports, lack of ability, poor instruction in early years, lack of focus on the basic skills, or a lack of attention to the mental side of sports.

Confidence in young athletes does not come automatically. It begins as a fragile thread of an attitude. It can be strengthened by proper development into a steel cable. Most of the reasons kids drop from a sport are because of a lack of properly developed skills and proficiency. When a kid believes he or she is bad at a sport, they don't have fun or gain confidence in themselves. But when we help them become confident in themselves and their abilities, they love their sport.

When kids have fun they want to come back (desire motivation). We have a strong role in making practices (and games) fun. Combining positive fun activities with physical proficiencies results in continued involvement and participation. Practices that work hard on physical development, proficiency, and having fun help kids improve their skills, and they don't dislike the repetitions. Continuous participation and internal drive grow into higher and higher levels of performance. These higher performance levels and skills are reinforced by the athlete inside (Mr. Victor), the coach, other players, parents, etc.

High performance creates self-confidence in the young athlete. This is performance-based *real* confidence, not just an external observer falsely telling a player they're good at something. Players know the real thing when they see it. Confidence comes in varying degrees from player to player and within a single player from day to day. Confidence is a tremendously powerful attribute for any athlete. We can see confidence in the way young athletes carry themselves and behave. Instilling and facilitating quiet self-confidence (not cockiness) into our players through positive, exciting practices will be one of our greatest accomplishments. Presenting her philosophy on confidence, Karlene Sugarman writes:

> True self-confidence is an athlete's realistic expectation about achieving success. These expectations are a big part of who you are and what you will or will not achieve. It's a state of being, a feeling about who you are and what you are capable of achieving. Success has nothing to do with what you *hope* to do, but what you realistically *expect* to do. Athletes with optimal self-confidence set realistic goals they can achieve and that will perpetuate their success. Even then, you need to have the skills and work hard to back up your confidence. All the self-confidence in the world can't replace the physical tools and knowledge essential for sports. (Sugarman, p. 177)

Here's one final thought on confidence. Confidence and self-esteem are two attitudes we hear much about. It seems we want kids to have a lot of both. High levels of confidence and self-esteem will give our young people the inner-strength to say "no" to a lot of life's temptations. Millions of kids give in to peer pressure because of a lack of confidence and self-esteem. Results include drug abuse, alcohol use, sexual activity, diminished academic performance, and a whole host of other negative outcomes.

We adults have a responsibility to help every athlete develop these important traits of confidence and self-esteem. You'll remember our earlier chapters that presented many different kinds of parents and coaches. Negative adult personalities and behaviors

create just the opposite goals. If adults consistently focus on negative aspects of a child's performance or attitude, the young athlete
cannot grow properly. Bad coaches create an environment that
holds kids back. Young people will not feel comfortable trying a
new skill. They will adopt a fear of failure as a result of ridicule by
coaches and parents. When adults use sarcasm and only focus on
the negatives, kids lose their inner desire to grow. And if they don't
grow and succeed, they won't develop high levels of confidence
and self-esteem. If kids are embarrassed by the behavior of their
parents, they become mentally focused on the wrong things and
rob themselves of a proper focus on their own involvement in their
sport.

Negative behavior by adults harms kids in many ways. Confidence and self-esteem are damaged. Kids need these things and
youth sports should offer them the opportunity to develop important lifelong attitudes. And one of the best ways to do this is through
positive practices and games coupled with solid adult reinforcement, support, and guidance.

Practices and Games

Practices

Our goal is to teach the mechanics of our particular sport in
practice sessions. Early in the practice season we should explain to
the team the philosophy of why we all practice. Most kids inher-
ently think they know why we practice. Take the time to explain
why drill and repetition are so important. Explain muscle memory
and conscious physical skills and mental focus. This will help kids
approach practices with the correct common goals and attitudes.
Also it's a good idea early in the practice season to develop a schedule of mechanical activities. You should coordinate the details with
your other coaches and set specific practice goals and drills. Have
all your practices build upon each other and continually advance
with more drills every practice session. You should keep this information in your calendar notebook, which contains all your other
individual player and team notes, goals, desires, favorite positions,
and more.

Pregame

Young athletes need to understand the importance of consistent pregame preparations, both mental and physical. Mentally, they should be thinking about the upcoming game in route to the field, court, or rink. They should be going over any game-related strategies the coach has explained. They should be reminding themselves of the positive mental aspects of the game and keeping Mr. Victor positive. This pregame forethought will create positive anticipation in the athlete and help avoid paralyzing negative pressure.

Physically, pregame warm-ups should be fairly consistent from game to game. Kids need some continuity in their otherwise ever-changing lives. The players will know what to expect and they can go through most warm-ups on their own. This will leave time for the coaches to tie up all the pregame loose ends. As the players control their own preparations, they also take control of their team attitude and performance. We covertly hand them the reins of the team, little by little and piece by piece.

Games

Regarding the entire physical aspect of mechanics and basic development, a game is not the place to work on individual skills. These basic skill techniques should already be in the subconscious muscle memory category. In his book *Empowering Children to Cope with Difficulty and Build Muscles for Mental Health*, author Eric Dlugokinski states:

> We usually think of muscles as parts of our body that contribute to our forcefulness, our stamina, and our vigor. Muscles provide the strength and power for motion. They develop gradually as we mature, and they need to be exercised consistently to reach their optimal potential.
>
> Analogous to these physical muscles are "mental muscles." We cannot see them, but they serve a function similar to physical muscles. They provide the strength for emotional health by serving as the raw materials for helping us move and relate effectively in the world around us. Similar to their

counterpart in the physical realm, they develop slowly and only with much practice and exercise. (Dlugokinski and Allen, p. 115)

On the mental side, there is one great mental mechanic every athlete should adopt. You can explain the goal and importance of this simple yet effective individual player thought. Between every baseball pitch, football snap, puck drop, tennis serve, or basketball play, the player should ask him- or herself this question: "What Do I Do If...?" Then depending on the sport, the player fills in the blank. Examples include:

▲ What do I do if the ball comes to me?
▲ What do I do if the puck comes to me?
▲ What do I do if the soccer player blocks me?
▲ What do I do if the running back comes my way?
▲ What do I do if the second serve is easy to return?
▲ What do I do if the wind is blowing left to right for my approach shot?
▲ What do I do if the ball does not come to me?
▲ What do I do if the play is to the other side of the field?

Many coaches develop hoarse voices by constantly yelling "reminders" to the players to think about individual situations. The acronym "WDIDI" (wadeedee) is a word young players can think alone and as a verbal reminder to fellow players. This single word automatically triggers game situation awareness in every player's mind without a coach having to lose his or her voice. There are many "What ifs." We must constantly remind every player to mentally focus on this individual thought until it becomes automatic. A benefit to the "What if" focus is the development of a unified group of players who keep their heads and minds in the game at all times.

Post-Game Discussions

What do you do after the game? Is your routine the same? Do you even have a routine following each game? Successful teams always have brief post-game recaps that focus on the physical and mental areas and overall game performance. Every coach is different and every game wrap-up will highlight a variety of points, but we can look at four separate situations that will pertain to any game.

The first situation is a team victory where the team has played their best. In this circumstance, it's easy to be positive. You can recount the physical and mental successes that helped provide the victory.

The second situation is a team victory but where the team did not play their best. These wins are hollow because of the lack of strong physical play or mental alertness. Coach discussions after these games should focus on the obvious areas of needed improvement that will be important for the next game.

The third situation exists when the team loses and has played badly. These are our most frustrating games emotionally and our most challenging games to identify areas of positive performance. But our job is to give a full recap, which includes any positive game aspects. The coach must also address areas where the team did not live up to its goals and expectations. Everyone usually feels pretty bad after these types of losses so you can be philosophical and remind all players it was not their best performance but they lost as a team and need to be prepared to show improvement for the next game.

The final game situation is a team loss but where the team played with solid physical and mental skills. No one can be upset if the team played its best and just happened to be behind when the game ended. During this discussion, you must remind the team of the important fact you have been stating all year: You want the team always to do its best regardless of the score. Remind the players of the successes from the game and they can hold their heads high because of their good performance.

Sample Practice

*Fund*amentals. Our practices must involve the elements of teaching the basics and *fun*. It is the fun aspect that keeps them coming back and enjoying the participation. Here is a typical practice session for baseball but it can be custom designed to fit your sport or conditions. You'll get the idea as you see the flow of activity. It's not perfect and is always changing slightly as we find successes and nonsuccesses. As coaches running these practices, we need to be flexible enough to modify our routines to accommodate players, skill needs, weather, etc.

Our practices need to be age appropriate. Two-hour sessions can be great for 13- to 17-year-olds but may be too long for 7- to 8-year-olds. You should ask players how long they would like to see their practices go. If you're doing your part, they'll enjoy longer practices. You must keep practices exciting and eliminate as much boredom as possible. Having a "station" type of format keeps many kids involved and constantly rotating from station to station. Be creative in your drills and keep them fast-paced. You should blend the practice routines with physical and mental practices. Work on both sides of the sport.

Typical Practice

Here's an outline for a typical two-hour baseball practice of 12- to 15-year-old boys. The practice season starts inside a gym, and we have a boom box playing music during physical drills. We start with stretching. Coaches talk while players are stretching. A different player leads stretches for each practice. The coach explains what we'll be doing during practice (usually the same basic repetitive drills but with a few special drills sprinkled in, such as double-play drills, running drills, relay catch races, etc).

Wall Drill (15 minutes)

The coach demonstrates proper body form and technique. Kids break into small groups and rotate throwing and catching grounders to a spot on a wall. Each player gets 150-175 catches and throws in 15 minutes

Coaches continually observe, monitor, and offer constructive reinforcement throughout the 15 minute rotation wall drill

Break (5 minutes)

Discuss the mental philosophy of (fill in the blank). Some examples could include: batting, handling pressure, base running, muscle memory, defense and offense, respecting umpires, fear and failure, limitations, quiet confidence, etc. You could substitute free throws, soccer defense, second tennis serves, the short game around

119

the green, regular season games versus tournament games, match play in golf, zone versus one-on-one coverage, or many other relevant topics.

Outfield Drill (15 minutes)

Demonstrate proper technique and line up in small groups. Coaches have six balls each and throw three to each player in line. Each throw is farther away. Players catch three and run back with the balls while the coach throws to the next player. Good physical coordination development and overall conditioning.

Break (5 minutes) (turn music down)

Base Running

You should be about half way through practice now. Pass out a treat (a chewy candy like Tootsie Roll Pops lasts several minutes and keeps players quiet). Explain the next drill: Base jumping from first and second with a mock pitcher on the mound. We have three players on each base taking a lead. The drill focuses on the runner's lead and the pitcher's motion so players develop the ability to get a good jump to steal a base or dive back to base. Do this until every player rotates 3 or 4 times. It takes about 10 minutes.

Hitting (15 to 20 minutes)

Demonstrate the finger grip and proper swing. Break into small groups using wiffle balls (baseball and golf ball sizes). Each player gets 10 swings, then rotates within the small group of tossers and shaggers. Each player will get 75 to 100 swings while the coaches wander around reinforcing, correcting, teaching, and helping. A good optional drill is a bunting exercise.

Last 15 to 20 minutes, live hitting (still in gym)

Two coaches throw wiffle baseballs (10 to each hitter then rotate). Coaches are in the middle of the gym and hitters are in opposite corners. Shaggers are scattered around the coaches feeding them balls. Keep this drill fast-paced.

This two-hour typical practice gives you the idea of what we are trying to accomplish. The players learn many basic skills, get a good workout, and have fun. A quick note: Common sense says if we use some sort of physical activity (like running laps) as discipline, kids begin to equate physical exercise with negativity. Our goal is to keep physical exercise in a more positive environment. We start baseball practice early in the year in a gym several months before we go outside. This helps protect young arms. By the time we get outside the players have thrown several thousand times and have swung a bat a few thousand times. When we do get outside, the practice drills get modified but we always focus on quick rotation and high repetition activities. We sprinkle in plenty of breaks (philosophical discussions) for mental development and fun. You and your other coaches can do the same and be creative with your practices. The kids will have more fun and so will you.

Visualization

One of the keys to physical improvement is to have a keen awareness of exactly how our bodies perform a task. We have to know what different parts of our bodies are doing before we can develop and improve our skills. Presenting a philosophy of visualization, Jerry Lynch offers the following:

> Visualization simply quiets and clears the mind of limiting thoughts and stops it from sabotaging your efforts so that your body is capable of doing what it has been trained to do. For example, you could be the most competent person on the team or candidate for the job. Negative self-talk and images create anxiety and tension, both of which block your efforts to perform up to your capabilities; visualization, on the other hand, clears the way for you to do all that is needed to complete the task successfully. It keeps you on track and maximizes your chances of positive results. It creates expectations of satisfaction, happiness and joy, and you respond by choosing the right people, situations and occurrences that fulfill those expectations. When you carry around

images of triumph and success, you create a state of inner calm, confidence and relaxation—all of which contribute to actual success. (Lynch and Huang, p. 22)

There are two kinds of visualization. The first deals with the eyes and what a player sees. We know they see many other athletes playing their sport and can witness different styles of physical performance. Many of the players on your team, however, do not know how they look while performing a specific skill. They think they know, but they don't. During an early practice session, set up a video camera and record each player in a variety of skill areas. You can review this video to identify opportunities to help each player.

Another use of the video is to show the players how they look. Most players will be surprised that what they see with their eyes does not match what they thought they saw in their minds. This review session with each player is a good time to point out skills being performed well and other constructive pointers. Once the player sees what you see, they'll be better able to understand and implement your suggestions. You might have each player bring their own videotape and you could record them several times throughout the practice and game seasons.

The second type of visualization is on the inside. One of our goals is to help the players develop this mental, visual, internal sense of how their bodies perform. There is one little drill you might want to consider in an effort to achieve this goal. During repetitive drills, have your players perform a skill with their eyes closed. Obviously you have to set up this exercise in a safe manner. The players will not be distracted by what they see with their eyes. They can physically do some task and get the "feel" internally of what they are doing. This might be something you try during routine stretching warm-ups on a few exercises. Something as simple as doing jumping-jacks or toe-touches with their eyes closed can help them "feel" what individual parts of their bodies are doing. It has potential merit for the players if they can enhance their awareness of their own bodies. From his book *Mastering Your Inner Game*, author David Kauss describes the mind/body relationship:

Mental rehearsal is one of the simplest, most tried-and-true methods of preparing to perform. It's straightforward and it works. The athlete goes through the physical performance in his or her mind, visualizing the body performing exactly as it's supposed to in competition. Mental rehearsal serves as a machinelike programming of the mind, which controls the body, to perform as planned. Because of this, mental rehearsal—the purest form of visualizing in the mind what the body will do—is often an excellent technique for athletes who tend to get caught up in patterns of positive or negative emotions, or both, before competitions. This technique can give you a stress-free, refreshingly direct alternative to your worry or to your confidence. If you tend to be negative, mental rehearsal can calm you through the knowledge that you've prepared yourself thoroughly to perform well. If you're already confident and positive in your emotional approach, mental rehearsal can provide the actual learning necessary for good performance. Physical practice is good; mental and physical practice prepares the whole self. (Kauss, p. 190)

We can also help players in this area of "visualization" while their bodies are still and relaxed. Beware, some people will think the kids are learning a form of Far-Eastern Zen Buddhism or Transcendental Meditation. Don't worry. Explain that many Olympic and professional athletes use a form of mental visualization to improve their performance and their mind/body connection. Just have the players sit in a relaxed position with their eyes closed. Tell them to take a few deep breaths and clear their minds so that they can visualize a situation you describe. They can look at themselves (like a bystander) achieving some goal or performing well and feel the associated levels of emotions and positive excitement. Visualization can be a powerful tool in our toolbox of guiding young athletes from the inside out.

Visualization is mental imagery that uses all the senses. You can use some degree of visualization with athletes of any age. Obviously, your approach with 10-year-old kids will be different than with 16-year-old teenagers, but with some creativity, you can get your kids thinking and "seeing" positive performance. There are complicated psychological theories and explanations why our bodies act out what we "see" in our minds. There have been many studies proving the power of visualization and mental imagery. Athletes from every sport will testify to the fantastic effects they have experienced in their performance because of their mental imagery sessions.

For kids of any age, have them relax quietly and visualize something simple. They should close their eyes and pretend they're seeing themselves performing a specific task. You can pick the task that fits your particular sport or activity. Depending on the age of your kids, you can make the visualization session as short or as long as your judgment believes is appropriate. With older teens, you can have them visualize a variety of skills and performance behaviors. The key, for any age person, is for them to see "in their mind's eye" themselves doing a task. Here are some examples:

▲ Have individual tennis players "see themselves" (like watching themselves in a movie) making a lot of first serves or making good return shots after rushing to the net.

▲ Have your baseball pitchers "see" the balls speeding over the lower inside quarter of the plate.

▲ Have your place-kickers "see" themselves making 10 field goals in a row from various distances.

▲ Have the goalies imagine themselves making excellent saves.

▲ Have your golfer visualize every shot, ball trajectory, flight, landing, and final resting place on the fairway or green.

▲ Have your soccer players "see" themselves making crisp accurate passes to their team members and scoring a goal.

▲ Have your track and field athletes "see" themselves jumping over the bar with ease or running comfortably around the track or long-distance course.

▲ Have your basketball players visualize themselves making 10 free throws in a row.

Examples are endless. But you get the idea. Of course, to utilize the powerful concept of visual imagery, you have to consider the ages of your athletes. But, because our bodies perform in the manner of our primary thoughts, it makes perfect sense to practice mental imagery and help our young people begin to use this excellent tool. Mental imagery can be practiced when they are alone in a quiet relaxed setting. Not to be confused with daydreaming, visualization incorporates all the senses and stimulates the body's muscles and brain to actually perform better.

To illustrate the incredible power of visualization, let's play a mental game. Right now, imagine in your mind an event that was emotionally powerful to you. Transfer your body to your first kiss or the birth of your first child or the time you were saying your wedding vows. Maybe select an unpleasant experience like your first broken bone, being dumped by an early boy- or girlfriend, or your first traffic ticket. Whether the event you select was incredibly positive or horribly negative, you can undoubtedly remember every fact like it occurred only yesterday. And you can relive the event with every sense of smell, sight, sound, and emotion. With this example, you can see how powerful visualization can be. It can encompass every fiber in your body and mind. Visualization can be equally powerful from past events that have already occurred, as well as projecting yourself to some imagined future event. Author David Kauss also writes:

> One good way to enhance your imagery powers and elevate them beyond mere thoughts is to focus on your five physical senses: sight, sound, smell, taste, and touch. Since we take in about 80 percent of our information about the world through our eyes, it's most important that you visualize your images, encouraging yourself to see them as vividly as possible.

> Imagery is most simply described as pictures in your mind. We all have the ability to imagine situations or events whether or not they have actually occurred. We can see in our mind's eye "movies" of events; we don't just think

thoughts about the event but can actually picture it unfolding, as it happened or could happen, inside the mind. (Kauss, p. 70)

It is easy to teach physical mechanics. It is harder to focus on the inside, but ultimately more rewarding. Coaching from the inside out does not come naturally for everyone. Some make it look easy. We all can improve. It is an ongoing process of molding each player and team (without them even knowing it) to achieve his or her maximum potential.

Chapter Highlights
to Improve Your Game Plan

▲ A coach must transform practices (which can be boring) into positive exciting learning opportunities.

▲ Repetitive skill drills begin with conscious effort and turn into subconscious muscle memory.

▲ With muscle memory, kids should "let" their bodies perform the skill instead of trying to "make" their bodies perform.

▲ Solid practices lead to higher levels of performance which lead to increased levels of confidence.

▲ Practices should be planned out and should be building blocks of skill development throughout the pre-game and game season.

▲ WDIDI (Wadeedee) is a mental habit whereby young athletes can keep their heads in their sport by the constant thought "What Do I Do If..."

▲ Athletes can visualize their physical performance and enhance their abilities.

CHAPTER 16

Teaching Values

It all starts on the inside

Think way back to your favorite teacher. It might have been a schoolteacher, a Sunday school teacher, a parent, a coach, or another important adult in your life. That person burned a lasting impression in your mind. They had an incredible impact on you, probably more than you realize.

The most important thing we do as adults is teach. Obviously we teach how to throw a ball, swing a club, hold a bat, make a free throw, make a slapshot, run the race, or make a free kick. We also teach important values kids will use for life. We help kids formulate long-lasting internal belief systems. We teach by word and we teach by example. Many of us underestimate the importance of our teaching roles and don't fully appreciate the huge impact we have on young people. Let's look at the major value-based lessons and internal attitudes we can help our young players learn and adopt.

Gut Optimism

Providing thoughts on the power of optimism, Les Brown writes:

Differing views and approaches to life can have a definite impact on the individual's quality of life, even on matters of health. Studies indicate that people who are more optimistic live longer and spend less time in the hospital than people who are pessimistic. The optimists have better relationships. The person who sees life in optimistic terms is much more willing to take life on in a dynamic way. (Brown, p. 41)

In athletic endeavors and all other aspects of life, it is important to have a strong inner sense of optimism. This is a core belief within a person's soul that they expect to be a winner in life. Winners with this consistent inner positive focus will avoid the paralyzing effects of perfectionism because they expect good things to occur in their sphere of life. They expect the best and believe they deserve the best. Winners realize instinctively that it is the negative belief of their own self-image, and not what they really are, that holds them back from achieving their maximum potential. Winners are not surprised by adversity; instead, they expect it, plan for it, and create possible solutions. In *Leading With the Heart*, Mike Krzyzewski offers his philosophy of a winner:

In order to be a winner, you have to look for ways of getting things done and not for reasons why things can't be done. People who live with excuses have things that can't be done hovering around them all the time. The only way we lose is if we don't try our best. (Krzyzewski, p. 232)

Science tells us that our bodies behave in a way consistent with our dominant thoughts. Winners are in control of Mr. Victor and their own internal self-belief system. To prove this, ask your young athletes to describe something they are good at and notice the positive words and attitudes presented. Gut optimism is the foundation for all the desirable traits of confidence, positive self-talk, inner drive, motivation, and mental control. Gut optimism becomes an unbreakable attitude and a way of life. Instead of fearing failure, optimism makes people look at risks and failures as opportunities to improve and perform. Optimists find the good in every situation. Positive attitudes become transferred into actions. As a coach or parent of young impressionable minds, and as you practice the philosophies of guiding kids from the inside out, you mold and develop the attitudinal seeds of true successful individuals.

Mental Focus

This is an excellent trait to have as a child or an adult. Some sports have more mental time available for thinking and getting bored than other sports. Players must learn to overcome getting bored and avoid letting their minds wander during a game. Mr. Victor needs to be involved in a positive way. Kids must use mental focus to be patient, especially in slow moving or low action games. We need to teach them mental exercises to use (like WDIDI, "What do I do if...?"). This will help them to avoid being sidetracked or distracted, to maintain peak levels of attention and performance until the game is over. Boredom and distraction are harmful and can creep into any game in obvious ways. Some examples include:

▲ The right fielder who rarely sees the ball because everyone is pulling balls to the left off a slow pitcher.

▲ The defensive soccer player while his offensive team is spending most of the game on the opponent's side of the field.

▲ The golfer walking to his ball for the next shot.

▲ All players on the bench or sideline.

All players on and off the field need to work at maintaining mental focus to keep their heads and bodies in the game from beginning to end. It stands to reason that a highly motivated player will spend more time than a lesser-motivated player thinking about the particular sport prior to an event. Mental focus is also the vehicle for the critical repetition of positive thoughts we all must practice to reinforce our internal positive beliefs. We must teach our players the value of believing in themselves and repeating the positive internal dialogue that will build strong positive self-images. An excellent way to do this is to build on every success or well-performed skill. Players must practice positive mental repeti-

129

tion. We all remember the child's story of the little choo-choo train climbing up the hill that kept saying, "I think I can, I think I can." Eventually the train found the inner-confidence to climb and conquer the hill. It all starts with optimistic positive repetitive self-talk.

Reaping the Rewards

Competing in an activity provides our young people with excellent opportunities for excitement and fun, plus competition offers valuable lessons for life. As children compete, they learn much about themselves and others. Our goal is to help them grow and mature through the vehicle of competitive sports. Carl Pickhardt states:

> Given the risks and challenges of competition, it takes a certain amount of self-esteem to be willing to compete. Fortunately, participation provides rewards that can make these risks and challenges feel worthwhile.
>
> • There is *fun* from enjoyment of the event itself: "I just like being able to get out there and play."
>
> • There is *satisfaction* from practicing skills and then putting them to the test: "I like getting better and then seeing how well I can do."
>
> • There is a sense of *belonging* from being part of a team or group: "I like the way we all work together."
>
> • There is *fulfillment* from trying one's hardest, win or lose: "I'm glad I gave it everything I had to give."
>
> • There is becoming absorbed in the *intensity* of performance: "When it's just me against an opponent, I really focus on myself."
>
> • There is *exhilaration* of defeating an opponent: "It feels great to beat the other team."
>
> All of these rewards are powerful enhancements to self-esteem. (Pickhardt, p. 72)

Sportsmanship

This critical value starts at the top and works its way down to the players. Coaches, who are in a highly visible position, demonstrate both good and bad sportsmanship. There's no middle ground. Parents also display good and bad sportsmanship. It's amazing what many young eyes and ears are exposed to and how they interpret these actions from grownups. We must show and promote a positive attitude to team players, especially if they are in a slump. Also we need to be polite and respectful to other teams, win or lose. Our good behaviors should also be extended to the umpires, referees, and judges. Remind every player they are representing their school, community, or organization. Their behavior is being judged constantly. In life, being a good sport is more important than being good at a sport.

Self-Control

The two kinds of self-control are emotional (internal) and physical (external) control. Emotional self-control relates to the voice inside our head that can help us. It is natural for a player to be upset when he or she does not live up to individual standards. And coaches constantly raise the bar with higher expectations. The key for you is to help the player accept temporary failure as a part of any sport and manage failure in the proper way (as we have already learned in an earlier chapter). You can help young athletes to control their emotions instead of allowing their emotions to control them. Do this by getting them to use immediate positive self-talk and allowing quick, short reactions to the situation. Have the player relax with a few deep breaths while reflecting on the event. Finally they should learn from the mistake, put it behind them, and get on with the performance.

Let's consider a typical example. Imagine a young player involved in an important competitive situation. This young person has worked hard to improve and has developed a high level of self-confidence because of his or her experiences of past positive performance. Then imagine this young person who, for whatever reason, has a bad day or performs badly over a period of several events. Frustration will set in. It's unavoidable. You can play an important role by teaching your young athlete to emotionally cope with his or her frustration. The key to helping young people develop and maintain healthy self-control is to teach them proper perspective about their own performance.

Physical self-control is related to the areas of sportsmanship and anger control. All players have to realize they are on stage in game situations. Negative player behavior hurts performance and reflects on the entire team, especially on the coaches. If you allow it and tolerate it, you appear to condone it. As a result you will then see more of it than is acceptable. Your best bet is to nip it in the bud early by stating your rules toward bad behavior and keep it from growing into a problem.

Self-Discipline

Self-discipline is different from the discipline in Chapter 12 that dealt with rules and regulations. We help players develop the individual discipline to do what is right in life. Through hard, fun work, they become disciplined in their dedication and physical habits as they see improved results. They become disciplined in their approach to good sportsmanship, pregame practices, teamwork, and persistence. They become *self*-disciplined. Mike Krzyzewski offers his thoughts on discipline:

> Some people feel that discipline is a dirty word, but it shouldn't be. All it really means is doing what you are supposed to do in the best possible manner at the time you are supposed to do it. And that's not such a bad thing.
>
> So our team has to be disciplined in their work. They have to participate in a conditioning routine because if they're not physically fit, fatigue sets in early. And when you're tired, you can start making mistakes. They must also have the discipline of physical habits. Then there's the discipline of good sportsmanship, of being patient, of being enthusiastic and energized every time out. And, of course, we have to instill the discipline of respect for authority, the discipline of

personal responsibility, and the discipline to be honest. (Krzyzewski, p. 46)

Responsibility

Responsibility is closely related to mental self-control. It is a desirable trait found in winners in every walk of life. We can help individual players develop personal responsibility by making them realize they alone control their athletic performance (and their entire life). The old saying is true: "Winners make it happen while losers let it happen." Winning athletes take responsibility for their attitudes, Mr. Victor, their level of desire, their goals, and their performance. Taking responsibility is defined as every player constantly evaluating individual and team performance and making necessary adjustments for improvement and success.

Motivation

In simple terms, Gary Mack writes:

> Motivation is a popular word, especially in sports. It comes from a Latin word meaning 'to move.' Athletes can move in one of two ways, either toward seeking pleasure (rewards) or toward avoiding pain (punishment). Motivation can be the desire to succeed or the fear of failure. (Mack, p. 88)

This value is an attribute we take with us in life. The ability to motivate ourselves and stay motivated is critical to our future jobs, academics, and relationships. True motivation must come from the inside. Youth sports provide an opportunity to develop this trait. We coaches and parents can help develop proper abilities. We can teach players how to take responsibility for their own inner drive and then channel it, control it, and use it to their benefit. When we bring fun back into practices and games, kids perform better with greater self-confidence. This creates an upward spiraling effect of stronger inner drive, higher performance, and even more confidence. On the subject of helping our kids to become positively motivated, Gary Mack offers another thought:

What we associate with pleasure we pursue. What we associate with pain we avoid. Playing sports as a kid should be an enjoyable, positive, and rewarding experience. But too often, impressionable youngsters are embarrassed by a coach, or they worry about pleasing their parents. Participating in sports then becomes a painful, even punishing experience. As a coach I would want my kids to have fun. I would want them to be eager and excited. I would want them to feel they are improving and focusing on the process rather than the outcome. (Mack, p. 90)

Language

Appropriate language by you and your team says a lot. Foul language should not be practiced or tolerated, period. Youth sports are no place for bad language by players, coaches, or parents. Not only is foul language bad for fans to see, it adds to negative thoughts, negative attitudes, and more negative behavior. It then grows into negative performance. As adults we need to help players channel frustration in more positive ways.

Team Spirit

Team unity and spirit are two of those contagious invisible factors that help teams rise to higher levels in game situations. Team spirit shows itself in the pride players have as a group when they represent their team and supporting organization. Team spirit is a strong result of friendships and bonds that occur naturally over time as a group of individuals becomes one unit. A comparison could be made to an army battalion that goes into a battle situation. This group of individuals comes out of the battle with a bond of having gone through something together and persevered. Your team goes into a game battle experience as a group and each person must do their part for the good of "their side," the team. Individuals must work side by side with others, some they may not even like, in order to help each other achieve a common goal. This is a great lesson for life.

Positive Persistence and Perseverance

The ability to "hang in for the long haul" and "stick it out" is powerful. Author Les Brown offers an example of its power:

> Remember when you learned to ride a bicycle? Or how about when you taught your own child to ride? All of that crashing into curbs, mailboxes, and parked cars sure looked like failure, didn't it? But in the end, we all learn to ride. We all want to get on and ride off right away, but few things in life happen that way. You don't become the master of something simply by attempting it. But you never become master of anything if you don't try. You have to have patience and persistence. (Brown, p. 51)

Attitude is everything. It drives a player to work hard and achieve individual goals of high performance. If given the choice between a player with potential and a strong 100 percent attitude, or a lazy superstar without the strong attitude, our preference is the kid with the strong attitude. A positive attitude of persistence and determination is contagious and visible to all. The desire in a player's belly to persevere in any circumstance translates into good motivation and higher expectations. For coaches it is easy to mold this player who is a pleasure to have on the team. The lesson for life with this type of persistent positive player is a "never quit" attitude. This player never says, "I can't."

Adjusting to Circumstances

Throughout life the ability to adjust is critical. We are all required to adjust to external and internal influences such as job, family, school, friends, and relationships. This is an important value to adopt in today's ever-changing environments.

In a single game, kids must constantly adjust to:

▲ A plate umpire's strike zone

▲ A soccer referee calling all contact as violations

▲ A football line judge calling all minor violations

▲ Picky basketball referees

▲ Weather conditions

▲ Trash talk from the opposing team

Players must be able to adjust in individual games to a variety of factors. They need to monitor the situations, be aware of the options, and make good decisions. Throughout the season, young players experience many changes that include new game positions, new coaches, and new teammates. Kids with positive self-images and confidence can work through any of these changes as new opportunities and challenges. Mike Krzyzewski summarizes with this thought:

> Both good and bad events will take place as the season progresses. When the bad stuff happens, I'm always looking for a way to turn it into something that will work for us. I believe a leader has to be positive about all the things that happen to his team. How can you turn unsuccessful things into successful things? Overcoming adversity is part of becoming successful. And dealing with losses, mistakes, and bad breaks is simply part of life. (Krzyzewski, p. 108)

Living With Unfairness

Coaches often treat players differently from one another. There are always favorites, pets, and others who get starting or key positions and treatment. Often, it seems like players of higher skill levels sit on the bench or sideline while players of lesser ability get to play. Most athletes who don't get to play experience internal feelings of unfairness whether justified or not. It hurts the player and it certainly hurts the athlete's parents. It's at these times that parents have the critical responsibility to help guide the young player through these emotional whitewater rapids without adding to the negative emotions by piling onto a particular coach or situation. If parents do vocalize their beliefs to or in front of the athlete, the negative emotions get confirmed and grow into resentment and hatred of the coach. These internally harbored emotions can keep the players from respecting the coaches and harm team spirit.

Players often develop genuine feelings of dislike for those athletes favored by their coaches.

A perfect example can be found in a quiet young person who has above-average ability, has a positive self-image, and believes he or she is a solid contributor to the team. This young athlete believes his or her hard work and positive performance will be noticed by the coaches and he or she will see appropriate playing time during competitive events. On the same team, there is another child who is slightly below the average performance of other players. This second child, however, tends to "brown nose" the coaches and ask for more playing time. He or she also has parents who spend a lot of time with the coaches. In a case like this, if the quiet child spends less time playing than the other child (of lesser skill) the quiet confident child will feel he or she is being treated unfairly. These feelings are genuine and powerful. They can dominate a child's mind-set and get in the way of positive team play and individual performance.

Here are a few options on how to deal with perceptions of "unfairness" whether legitimate or not. In today's society of parents with strong protective desires, often a parent approaches a coach to find out why their child is being treated in a particular way. If the parent is calm, the discussion usually involves the coach explaining why an individual kid is not playing in the position he or she prefers. Often, however, the parent is upset and emotional and we all know those discussions are rarely productive.

The best option, if any action is going to be taken at all, is for the young athlete to calmly ask the coach for a one-on-one discussion. The athlete can explain his or her perception about the current situation and inquire why things seem "unfair." Most every coach will respect the young athlete behaving in such a rational "adult" manner and have a good conversation. These talks usually end with the young player feeling better about having talked personally to the coach. The player often learns "constructive criticism" of his or her own performance or attitude that may be playing a part in the current perceived situation of "unfairness." There are no guarantees the coach will immediately change the situation but the player will have communicated in an adult way. The player will learn how to address various types of unfair situations for a particular sport and for life in general.

We've looked at some of the important values and character traits we instill in our young athletes. The next chapter highlights the negative side of being a youth sports coach.

Chapter Highlights
to Improve Your Game Plan

▲ Coaches and parents teach many life-long values by word and by example.

▲ Optimism within each young athlete is one of the most important traits we can help kids to learn.

▲ Coaches help kids learn the important values of sportsmanship, self-control, self-discipline, responsibility, motivation, and persistence.

CHAPTER 17

The Negatives of Coaching

Lots to think about and know

Help Wanted: Youth Coach

Job Requirements: Must work with all kinds of kids, drive kids around, feed kids, be a medical expert, be a communications expert, have conflict resolution skills, be a finance wizard, be a group counselor, statistician, physical therapist, event coordinator and gear repair expert, be thick-skinned, be an amateur weather forecaster, teacher, trainer, substitute parent, leader, helper, and friendly. Must have multiple skills in every area and a willingness to learn. Apply in person.

Coaching is not easy. If it were, anybody could do it. It takes special people with special gifts to dedicate ourselves to groups of young people. When we sign up to accept this crazy job we must have our eyes wide open and know what we're getting ourselves into. This chapter highlights a bunch of potentially negative factors we all need to be mindful of. Also it is good for all parents to be aware of the negatives and positives in coaching. The next few chapters will offer a variety of considerations. Coaches wear many hats, as you will learn. In his book *Sports in Society*, Jay Coakley gives us a broad view of coaching:

Coaching behavior, though it certainly reflects the traits and wishes of coaches themselves, is influenced by a combination of cultural beliefs about coaching and coaches, the organizational settings in which coaches work, and coaches' social relationships. The fact that coaches are held totally accountable for unpredictable outcomes of sport events creates pressure in their lives. This pressure is intensified by the public nature of sports and by the ease with which the competitive successes and failures of coaches can be measured. Coaches also have to contend with the strains created by dealing with so many different relationships while performing their jobs. The fact that expectations vary from one relationship to the next makes it difficult to keep everyone happy. (Coakley, p. 206)

Time Requirements

As coaches, we give huge amounts of our time to the commitment of coaching. Unless someone has been a dedicated coach themselves they have no idea of the time required and given to this task. We spend time individually and with our other coaches strategizing on how to run successful practices and games. We devote time to thinking about and discussing the players. We spend time developing team goals and rules. Obviously it takes time to get ready for and run practices. Also there are games and the associated pregame and post-game time requirements. And there is time given to parents in individual conversations and also in parent group settings. For most coaches there is also record-keeping time and roster and line-up development time.

Second-Guessing

Often you'll call a play based on probabilities, a gut feeling, player ability, or just the phases of the moon. Sometimes the play works and you're brilliant. Other times it does not work and unknowing parents think you're a fool. We open up ourselves to second-guessing by choosing the players who start and the positions they play. Whether we make a mistake or not, there will always be second-guessing. Let's imagine a typical situation. Imagine you and your team are locked in a close competitive event. It's crunch time and you make a decision to substitute a particular player or gamble with a somewhat risky play. Now suppose your decision backfires and fails. Even though you weighed all the probable outcomes, situations did not go in your favor. So what. You had your own reasons and will take responsibility. It's that simple. But you know there will be parents and athletes who will question your judgment. It's an expected part of your coaching responsibilities. On the topic of second-guessing and decision-making, Mike Krzyzewski writes:

> A leader has to have the courage to make a key decision in a split second. And then he has to have the courage to live with it afterward—whether it succeeds or fails. Because if he doesn't, he'll be afraid to make the next key decision. Courage and confidence are what decision-making is all about. (Krzyzewski, p. 113)

Talent Scout/Fortune Teller

Kids grow up and physically mature at varying rates. With a snapshot in time, in a given season, there's no way to know how a young athlete will look in a year or two. Today's uncoordinated klutz could transform into tomorrow's gifted athlete. Coaches are expected to recognize hidden potential and talent in all kids. All sporting programs and organizations want these oustanding kids to remain involved in the sport so when they do advance physically, they will still have the desire to play. A coach is expected to identify all future talent and then make sure the kids stay active. It's a hard thing to do.

Compassion Fatigue

This is a symptom known as mental burnout. People heavily involved inside other people's minds for long periods of time give so much of themselves; there's nothing else to give at the end of the day. Good examples are psychotherapists, the clergy, and various counselors. For kids at any given age, their emotional maturity can range two to four years in either direction. So a coach is dealing with a wide variety of emotional levels. Being a coach from the inside out is hard work and we become subject to mental fatigue. Good coaches truly care about their players. They expend much effort to know each player and help him or her grow. This focus takes a lot of time and mental energy.

141

Irate Parents

We've all had them. Unfortunately they are part of the game. These parents will call us at our homes to complain and/or give us their wisdom. Some provoke confrontations with coaches. Some engage in backstabbing (and second-guessing), which we cannot respond to. The major problem with negative vocal parents is that they often don't hide their feelings from their kids. This hurts our long-term efforts with the players and could undo our positive mental coaching work.

Youth sporting seasons are limited in time. It takes a lot of work to effectively guide young athletes from the inside out. Coaches have a short window of opportunity to help each young athlete. Throughout the ongoing process, the last thing a coach needs is a parent undermining the coach's good work. A parent can do damage by complaining in front of their child. It creates doubt in the young person's mind and the child will adopt the parent's negative attitude. When this happens, the coach is no longer effective in the positive mental development of the player.

Family Time

Coaching activities demand time away from our families. Often we coaches have a family member on the team, but many times we do not. Either way, coaching cuts into the time we could otherwise be spending with our families.

Glorified Babysitter and Taxi Service

We've all seen parents who consider us as babysitters and simply want to drop off their son or daughter for us to take care of. These parents look at our sporting activity as a time to clean the house, mow the lawn, or have some free time.

Also many coaches pick up and drop off kids for practices and games. Sometimes this is unavoidable but a regular habit begins to make us feel like we're being taken advantage of. If you don't want to be a taxi service you need to communicate travel responsibilities early in the practice season. The players will contact each other instead of you for rides.

Gear and Equipment Maintenance Expert

We keep the gear. We lug it around to practices and games.

With all this lifting, not only do we get free bodybuilding exercise workouts, we also get to monitor and repair equipment. Like it or not this ends up being one of our many responsibilities.

Fund Raiser

All groups need money for a variety of reasons (equipment, tournaments, trophies, picnics, uniforms, etc.). We all want the best for our players. As coaches we are the first to see the need for various expenditures. Consequently, we get involved in fundraisers.

Group Counselor

As coaches we periodically find ourselves involved in internal team personality conflicts (fights). You need to address these head-on. Get the players together to verbally identify the cause(s) of the problem and inquire as to possible solutions. Get those involved to cooperatively suggest the best outcome for the benefit of each person and the team. You can use the experience as a lesson to the team on why fighting can be natural with groups of kids and different personalities, but as a team it is negative. Explain we need to put these events behind us, learn from them and get on with the team's goals and objectives. The kids usually cool down and get over it. In her book, *From Conflict to Cooperation*, author Beverly Potter states that conflict can be beneficial for the team:

> Conflict itself is not a problem. It is a signal that an adjustment is needed. While solving the conflict presents the opportunity for people to clarify expectations, build cohesiveness, and create a problem-solving atmosphere, these benefits are not guaranteed. Achieving positive results does not come by chance—conflict must be well managed. Unfortunately, more often than not, it is poorly managed. A mishandled squabble can undermine team spirit and demotivate people. (Potter, p. 4)

Financial Reward

Most coaches volunteer so there is no money paid for services. Some get minimal pay in certain groups or schools. But even for the people who get paid a small amount of money, considering all the time dedicated to good coaching, they probably end up earning about 20 cents per hour.

Coaching Your Own Child

Approximately 70 to 80 percent of all coaches have their own child on their team. This presents a few warnings. Coaches tend to be either too lenient or too strict on their own kid. If they are too strict, they are trying to send a message to the rest of the team. They unfairly use their son or daughter as a lesson for the others.

Sometimes other coaches will let their own kid do things they would not tolerate in other players. All players notice this inconsistent treatment immediately and resent the coach for it. Some coaches showcase their own kid believing he or she is the superstar of the team. This coach believes that just because coaching is such a commitment, the coach's kid deserves special treatment. Not only will other players dislike the coach, they may be negative toward the coach's child.

All these situations need to be avoided from the start. The solution is to treat all players the same. You must be consistent and fair and remind yourself to treat your own kid just like any other player.

Coach's Thumbs

This is a muscle/joint problem we experience by standing for long hours with our hands on our hips. Over the season we put a lot of stretching pressure on our thumbs and related forearm muscles. The resulting symptoms are similar to arthritis with sore muscles. Try folding your arms or letting them just hang at your sides. But beware: Before you know it, those hands will be back on your hips.

Phone Calls

We seem to be constantly on the phone. We call all the players for practice changes and rainouts. We call for game reschedules. There are various reminders that need to be communicated to the team. You should split up the names and get your other coaches to share in the phone duties.

Wow! There are a lot of negatives. It's amazing our youth sporting programs get anyone to sign up as a coach. But as you'll see in the next chapter, there are many incredible positive aspects of being a youth coach.

CHAPTER 18

The Positives of Coaching

Many tremendous rewards

Help Wanted: Youth Coach

Job Requirements: Loves to work with kids, possesses the ability to help many kids grow into young adults, can teach kids about life, desires positive lifelong friendships, will contribute to humanity, will instill positive values in today's youth, wants to treasure the opportunity to help kids. Apply in person.

If you still want to be a youth coach and haven't thrown this book away after reading the negatives, you have what it takes. Coaching youth sports will be one of the most rewarding endeavors you undertake. Here are some of the positive aspects.

Many Into One

At your first practice, you usually see a variety of kids. Many of them don't know each other. You probably don't know the attitudes or skill levels of every child. Throughout the preseason and game season, you will become instrumental in creating a unique team. As you succeed in your quest, it is rewarding to see many separate individual kids at the beginning of the practice season grow into a single entity. As a coach, you are part of this growth and the overall team-building success.

Group Dynamics

In youth sports, kids from all backgrounds unite for a single purpose. They are forced to interact and spend a lot of time together. Kids travel together. Subgroups within the team often practice together. Offenses practice offensive skills. Defenses work on defensive tactics. Individuals work with other individuals on special skills. Relationships begin and as a coach, it is enjoyable to witness the bonds and friendships that develop.

Individual Growth

It is an incredible challenge to mold young people. Author Les Brown gives us his philosophy:

> The only way to push someone up a ladder is to climb with them, and so when you help others, your own life benefits. When we tune into the needs of others, we fulfill a vital spiritual need to be of service to others, and we also serve as an example for others to follow. When we teach by example that helping is good, we create more helpers and the good within us grows around us. (Brown, p. 62)

We get to help players grow in two ways. The first is physical growth, which includes skill advancement and strong basics. With a focus on positive practice drills and general healthy habits, we help kids improve physically. The second is mental growth. This includes the areas of confidence, fun, desire, and motivation. As coaches focusing on the insides of all our players, we will instill important attitudinal habits for life. Every child will benefit from our efforts.

Memories

We are part of long-term lasting memories being created in our players. When they look back at their time with us, we should be remembered in positive ways. We will have a lasting impact on many of the kids. Sporting activities become positive memories in which players enjoy the entire experience and their own participation.

Confidence

Helping to build confidence in young people is a positive aspect of being a coach. When we conduct positive exciting fun practices, players develop strong basic skills. As a result, they perform well and their confidence grows. Confidence is one of the greatest gifts we can give young players.

Long-Term Respect

During the short time we have young people loaned to us, our positive behavior burns lasting memories into their minds. As we focus on the insides of each player and the entire team, we will be a strong influence to every athlete. Years down the road, as grownups these individuals will remember us with appreciation and respect. Kids are impressionable and as adults they will realize we have played a positive part in many of their lives.

Part of Something Good

As coaches we have an internal sense of supporting the community, school, or organization. The efforts by these groups are positive to many people and the team. Our role as coach is being part of this long-term beneficial community influence. Coaches can be proud of their contributions made to the kids and the community.

Meeting Good Parents

Overall most parents are positive and supportive of our efforts. They want the best for their kid (just like we do). Our responsibility in this coach/parent relationship is to communicate clearly and whenever necessary so the parents understand our mutual goals with the team and how we are trying to achieve those goals. Most parents will look up to us and appreciate our desire to invest time and enable their kids to experience youth sporting activities.

Meeting Good Young People

Today's youth gets a lot of negative press. We frequently are exposed to the negative behaviors of kids all across the country. When we sign up to coach teams of youth athletes, we get the great experience of interacting with many good kids. This is one of the many rewards we receive.

Coaching Your Own Child

Many of us entered (and remain in) coaching because we have a son or daughter involved in a sporting activity. Our involvement creates some great memories in our kids' lives. They will have a long-term appreciation of what we do as a coach for them and their friends on the team. We experience a tremendous satisfaction and joy as our own kids sincerely thank us for being their coach.

Chapter Highlights
to Improve Your Game Plan

▲ Coaches expose themselves to many negative ramifications.

▲ Negative examples include time away from family, being second-guessed, mental burnout, dealing with upset parents, being a babysitter, and sometimes a fight referee.

▲ Coaching offers many rewards.

▲ Examples include turning many kids into one united team, helping individuals grow, making positive memories, building individual confidence in kids, meeting good parents, and sharing something good with their own child.

CHAPTER 19

Boys Versus Girls

Differences and how to help them all

The next statement should not shock any of you: Boys and girls are different. Not only are they a little different, they are very different. And because they are so different, as a coach or parent, we must understand why and how they are different.

Many factors affect young boys and girls. Much of their behavior and personality is pre-determined at birth through genetics. But in our society, other external factors mold the individual personalities of every young child. As coaches and parents, we cannot control every aspect of a child's environment as they grow into young adulthood. But we can and must at least be aware of the many forces kids experience. Our job is to recognize the world of our young boys and girls and then to operate within their worlds in positive, helpful ways.

Please do not let yourself misinterpret and get upset by statements and observations in this chapter. There is no intention to single out any individual of either sex. The statements made here are generalities we coaches and parents must consider as we deal with boys or girls. There are differences in the way each approaches the various aspects of youth sports. The following generalizations will apply to the larger overall groups of boys or girls. Within each group there will be exceptions to any broad observation or rule. As coaches we have to be aware of general differences so we can work within the team's personality to help each individual player and the team grow to its maximum potential. As parents, we must realize how differently boys and girls relate to youth sports. Regardless if you have boys or girls, your focus can be the same. Your focus can be on the inside. Girls' teams play other girls' teams and boys play other boys so the playing field is physically equal. Our job is to work on the inside and use our skills to develop and mold our teams.

Boys

Ages

From roughly five to nine years old, young boys are usually uncoordinated and have short attention spans. They focus heavily on fun. They experience all the early motivational factors detailed in this book. Practices are most effective in this age group if kept relatively short (45 to 60 minutes). From ages 10 to 14 years, boys become quite impressionable. They generally become quite knowledgeable about sports and are exposed to many different aspects of sporting. This age group can be teachable if we properly take advantage of coaching on the inside. From 15 to 18, young men should have more maturity. They have bigger-picture outlooks concerning their involvement in sporting activities. They also can better understand why we coaches do the things we do.

Hormones

This is the puberty stuff we've all experienced in various ways. There are physical and emotional considerations. Within a single age group (for example, 13-year-olds), maturity can vary three to four years. This is quite a span of emotional levels to work with. Other obvious differences include deeper voices, body hair, muscle expansion, etc. As a coach you can and should discuss the differences every boy will experience—without making fun of it. By the time they're 18, they all will have gone through the puberty thing.

Offering his thoughts on the effects of puberty, author Richard Bromfield writes in his book *Handle With Care*:

> What a wrench this puberty throws into the works of children, as if growing up isn't hard enough. Now, on top of every other thing they contend with, they have to feel their bodies heating up and doing all sorts of things they aren't used to. So much of the time they still feel like little kids who want to sit on their parents' laps, and yet, with every music video that passes, they are looking, sounding, and even smelling more like adults. (Bromfield, p. 45)

Personalities

We covered individual types and different personality traits in Chapter 8. We coaches get to deal with every characteristic regardless if our team is made up of girls, boys, or both. Any kid can be a natural confident athlete and any kid can be a cocky head case. We get a cross-section of people when we coach.

Egos

Ask almost any woman to define the male ego and she'll tell you that regardless of his age, most males are the same. Whether a male is five, 10, or 40, his ego can be loud and boastful on the outside. Yet, it can be fragile on the inside. She'll say males get their feelings hurt easily and are overly hard on themselves. She'll tell you the male ego is like a raw egg in the shell that must be handled delicately and with a lot of care.

Competitive Drive

From five to nine years old, little boys have a fledgling idea of competition. In 10- to 14-year-olds the attitude toward competition is in full force and everything becomes competitive. Relationships with teammates, siblings, friends, parents, teachers, and many others become competitive. At age 15 (plus or minus) competition becomes a major focus.

Historically, boys have tended to be more competitive as a whole. One boy will strive to beat another boy for a spot on the line-up, team, or starting position. Boys accept this competition among each other and begin to understand competition and the idea of winning and losing at earlier ages than girls. Most of us can identify individual girls who are very competitive, more than many boys. But in general and as a sex, boys are more competitive.

Boys are driven by their image and how they look among friends and to girls. They also are driven by a strong fear of failure (this is tied into that fragile ego). Boys don't want to lose. They associate losing with failure and are more focused on winning. Testosterone is a strong component that shows up early in a boy's life. It remains a powerful force for the rest of their lives and as we all know it surfaces in many ways.

Our job is to be aware of all these male factors and be prepared to deal with each area as it arises. Being empathetic to what a young boy is going through and having open communication are the best ways to stay in front of any potential problems.

Girls

Ages

From five to nine (or thereabouts), young girls are similar to young boys and their focus is primarily on having fun. At about 10 until 14 years of age, they express an increased level of drive and motivation. From age 15 (plus or minus) we see an increase in the competitive drive in girls. This competitive drive is found in individual situations and as a competitive team.

Hormones

Just as with boys, this puberty stage can vary greatly among girls of equal ages. There are many physical and emotional changes occurring within each girl that we coaches need to be cognizant of. Hormones in girls and boys are strong forces and are part of the natural growth process.

Personalities

Like boys, girls have many different personalities. They are all unique and we as coaches will see all personality types. As we focus on the inside of each player and the team, these separate personalities will come together to accomplish the predetermined team goals.

Egos

Girls do not have egos similar to those found in boys. A girl's self-worth is not as contingent on sports excellence as a boy's. Girls look in the mirror and do not judge success or failure on hitting a home run or making the winning play. Whereas boys place great importance on their own athletic performance, a girl's ego is based on a broader range of considerations. In general, girls do not live or die because of their athletic prowess. They often base their self-worth on positive relationships, physical appearance, and intelligence. Media advertising companies spend millions convincing young girls that physical appearance is the number one factor in their lives. Young female athletes have egos, but their egos are more diverse than the single-focus male egos.

Competitive Drive

As a rule girls are less competitive than boys. Girls tend not to have such a strong desire to beat their friend for a special spot on the team. Boys accept this "friendly competition" as natural, girls do not. Girls have a lesser focus on winning than boys of a similar age. In practice and game situations, girls are more concerned and aware of their appearance than boys are. Girls have a stronger drive to be with friends than boys do. Also, girls have a heightened sense of fairness as it pertains to competition and personal treatment of others. As an example, it is not uncommon for girls to focus less on their own performance than on how the other girl might feel. Girls are often more intuitive to other people's feelings and make decisions accordingly. In *Keys to Developing Your Child's Self-Esteem*, Carl Pickhardt writes about boy/girl differences:

> Parents should be aware of some traditional sex role definitions that still have some bearing on how male and female children can be socialized differently to develop their self-esteem. Boys often tend to define their worth primarily based on how they perform, doing well (achieving) as a major pillar of self-esteem. Girls often tend to define their worth primarily based on how they relate, being liked (socially connecting) as a major pillar of self-esteem. (Pickhardt, p. 101)

Coed

Having boys and girls on the same team is a relatively new phenomenon. It is found in soccer and other youth sports. This chapter is not going to deal with the societal rightness or wrongness of this politically correct topic. We'll focus our analysis on potential pitfalls you as a coach must be aware of if you have a coed team.

A coed team offers new challenges. One thing to beware of is inter-sex teasing. We all know kids can be mean if they want to be. Here are a few things to watch for:

▲ Boys might resent having to "play with the girls."

▲ Girls can resent the boys' hogging the ball all the time just to show off.

▲ Some boys might want to gently hurt the girl just to show them they can't play with "us stronger sex."

▲ Some boys might minimize performance by decreasing their aggressiveness and avoid any potential situation in which a girl could get hurt because boys are not supposed to hurt girls.

▲ Some girls will try so hard just to be equal to the boys, they use bad judgment and risk personal injury.

▲ Some girls realize they are not as athletic as most others on the team and develop a lack of confidence.

Keeping in mind different generalized motivations, boys and girls will want different things from their participation in youth sports. If you have a coed team, your focus can be similar to a single sex team but you need to keep the above pitfall situations in mind and watch for these "boy versus girl" interactions and attitudes. Make sure you have a team talk with everyone and advise them of certain behaviors you will not allow (like those mentioned above). Focus on the team attitude and team philosophy. And unless absolutely necessary, it's probably unwise to split the team by sex and have a talk with the girls and a talk with the boys. This promotes a separation and goes against your team development goals. If there are negative behaviors by certain individuals, you need to address the situation like any other problem requiring your attention.

Male and Female Coaches

Every coach is different regardless of his or her sex. We will not make any distinctions in this book based on the coach's sex. All coaches, male or female, should obviously bone up on the physical and mechanical aspects of the particular sport so you can be of the most benefit to facilitate team improvement. Male and female coaches alike should be aware of the differences between young boys and girls as well as their own styles, strengths, and weaknesses. Whatever you are, you can improve your success and help the team by incorporating the philosophies of coaching from the inside out. We're all different but we all can have a common thread of how we approach our coaching responsibilities.

So whether you coach a coed team, an all-boys team or an all-girls team, there are rewards and challenges inherent in each. As coach you'll experience many situations and be involved in many memorable experiences. If you incorporate the practices of molding young athletes from the inside out, your days and nights as a youth coach will stay with you as a positive personal force for a long time.

Next we take a look at how to deal with another factor of youth sporting teams, adult expectations, and communications.

Chapter Highlights
to Improve Your Game Plan

▲ Boys and girls are different and approach youth sports with different motivations and personality traits.

▲ Boys generally tend to be more competitive than girls and are motivated to succeed for different reasons than girls.

▲ Co-ed teams present unique challenges for coaches and players.

CHAPTER 20

Adult to Adult

How to interact for the good of our kids

In today's society many parents are actively involved in the lives (including sports) of their kids. Many have suggestions that are of great benefit to a coach. As a parent, you're way ahead of the game by simply reading this book. As a coach, you should solicit all parents' support by having them read this book to help you focus on and support inside-out coaching techniques. Years ago there was little parental involvement (except in school events). Today's greater visibility by parents can be positive if channeled properly, if they behave in such a way as to be positive to the coaches, positive to other parents, positive to officials, and positive to their own kids. Chapter 5 detailed the different types of parents and what motivates them. And Chapter 6 presented different kinds of coaches and their unique personalities. This chapter looks at ways to avoid many problems before they start, and if you do experience them, how to handle each situation for the betterment of all involved.

Communications

Up-front early communications are critical in this entire area of adult behavior and our impact on the kids. Coaches and parents must have a preseason group meeting for introductions and information. Coaches, players, and parents should introduce themselves to one another (they'll be spending a lot of time together). In this meeting, coaches should state the coaching philosophies, goals for the players, and goals for the team. Discuss first-aid equipment and procedures and determine if any parent has medical training. Make sure someone can bring a cellphone to the games in case of an emergency. For you coaches, hand out written or typed paperwork confirming the information you are presenting. Go through in detail the "Expectations" section in this chapter. Reinforce the strong positive role all parents have in the long-term development of their kids and the team. Solicit their support and help early in the season. This early meeting should end with an open question-and-answer session.

For you parents, don't ignore the importance of early communication with the coaches and other parents. If your child's coach does not organize a group meeting, request one. You may have to put together a list of various expectations for the meeting. The key is to lay some groundwork for acceptable adult behavior and create a dialogue for future communications.

Expectations

During the early group meeting, a handout with various expectations is appropriate. The expectations should be from the perspective of the coach, the parents, and the players. Parents and coaches should understand and attempt to live up to all expectations. The following is a sample basic list of expectations that can be tailored to fit your individual team/sport needs.

Coach expectations of parents

▲ Transportation to games and practices
▲ Help learn the basic fundamental mechanics and reinforce at home
▲ Have your child do various repetitive drills at home
▲ Arrive to practice and games on time
▲ Positive behavior at games
▲ Notify the coach of any medical or health problems

Coach expectations of players

▲ No profanity

▲ No disrespect to anyone

▲ Good sportsmanship

▲ Win and lose like winners

▲ Learn at practices and practice at home

▲ Attend all practices

▲ Call if you'll miss a practice or a game

▲ Remember that unexcused misses are not fair to the player or the teammates and may result in bench time

▲ Bring your own water

▲ Bring a willingness to learn, work hard, and have fun

Parent's expectations of coaches

▲ Practices will be exciting and focus on the basics—mechanical skills and mental skills

▲ Players will be treated fairly and consistently

▲ Coaches won't use profanity or abuse alcohol

▲ Criticism will be focused on correction of a skill and not the child

▲ Coaches will communicate regularly about schedules, home practice tips, helpful suggestions, equipment, etc

▲ Coaches will help players grow and mature in individual achievement, self-esteem, teamwork, and group support

▲ Coaches will focus on doing one's best, not just winning

Kids' expectations of coaches

▲ Help them learn

▲ Fun environment

▲ No criticism of the player, but corrections to improve are okay

▲ Rational behavior

▲ Keep practices exciting

▲ Professional behavior at games

Players' expectations of parents

▲ Get them to games and practices on time
▲ Wash their clothes
▲ Be supportive
▲ Be a good parent fan
▲ Remind them to bring sporting gear and a good attitude
▲ Play with them at home

Problems and grievances

▲ Discuss issues as adults
▲ Conduct open two-way communications
▲ Be open-minded to other views
▲ Consider the possibility you might be wrong
▲ Remember why we are all here (for the kids)
▲ Fairness and honesty

You can see from the above sample handout that there is a lot to cover in an early group meeting. But don't ignore this fantastic opportunity to discuss many critical topics and start a positive dialogue. Author Beverly Potter presents the benefits of early communications:

> It's amazing how often we are unclear about what others expect, which can result in working hard to satisfy a spouse or supervisor, only to fail because we've focused our efforts in the wrong place or in the wrong way. Unclear expectations can lead to misunderstandings and disappointments that fuel conflict. It is easier to get along with other people— even people you don't like or who are very different from you or whose priorities are divergent from yours—when you know what they expect of you and what you can expect of them. (Potter, p. 3)

Here's one final point on expectations: For you coaches, it is a good idea to clearly state to all parents that when their child is with you on the field, court, rink, or diamond, their child temporarily becomes your child. Express that any communication from the parent to their child should be limited and must be positive, period. Game situations are not the time or the place for negative criticism from parents. That would be counterproductive to the coach's goals.

Negative Parent Behavior

Sometimes a parent will violate the rules of sportsmanship. Some parents will behave inappropriately. If and when these situations arise, your role as coach offers you the authority figure responsibility to calmly ask the parent to adjust their behavior. We all can get carried away in particular situations and temporarily lose our heads. If you state the problem situation to the parent, your involvement usually ends the negative behavior. However, if negative parent behavior gets repeated, you will have to handle the parent in stronger terms. You may even have to ask the parent/violator to leave the game or stop coming to the games. Remember that negative parent behavior goes against the basic tenets of positive coaching from the inside out. We coaches must oversee all activities and often find ourselves dealing with the (temporary) immaturity of "adults." You might remind the parents in the early preseason meeting they are representing the community, school, or organization—just like the players.

Negative Coach Behavior

Periodically, in your role as a parent, you might witness a pattern of negative coach behavior. Examples could include violations of the expectations we just covered. In these circumstances, a rational adult conversation with the coach will usually help resolve the issue. If the behavior continues, you may need to have a meeting with other parents and the coach. You should restate your complaint to the coach and strongly urge him or her to reconsider their behavior or actions.

If the problem becomes serious, or if the coach refuses to change the negative behavior, you may be forced to elevate the issue. Most organized sports are controlled by a group or a formal organization or school. You as parents may have to present your case to the governing authority. By doing this, they will have to deal with the problem coach. This action is to be taken only after all other options have been exhausted. On this subject of negative adult behavior, Carl Pickhardt comments:

> Caught up in the competition, parents themselves can be a source of harm to their child's self-esteem. Either as coach or spectator, they can become over-involved to their child's cost. They can actually engage in punitive coaching, which is usually most destructive when it comes from a parent. Or as spectators, they can yell criticism of their child's play, or even loudly attack a referee for a call with which they disagree. In either case, they can be a serious embarrassment to their child, turning what was a positive experience for a child into one that feels bad. (Pickhardt, p. 74)

Remember, our responsibility is to our kids and all kids. None of us want to address these types of problems, but through the years of youth sports, they often become inevitable. If we adults conduct ourselves according to the expectations, problems should be minimal. By having an early group meeting, addressing and resolving problems becomes easier.

Let's restate a point. We all know most parents and coaches behave in positive supportive ways. Actually, coaches usually have limited interaction with parents. Both groups have a common goal of helping young people develop and grow. Our focus is on the kids and the team.

Chapter Highlights
to Improve Your Game Plan

▲ In the practice season, coaches and parents should discuss all expectations.

▲ Negative coaching behavior and negative parent behavior must be dealt with to allow the kids to have positive experiences.

SECTION V

The Season

Notes and Thoughts

CHAPTER 21

The Beginning

Here's where it all starts, much to do

Last season ended too quickly. It seemed like things were just starting to click. The kids were performing well. They were having fun and had bonded as a group. The parents and coaches were comfortable with each other. Then poof, the season was over. And now you are beginning to think about the next season. As they say, there's no time like the present—so you'd better get started.

Before the very first practice, there is much to do. There are many areas to cover in order to have a team well prepared for the game season. As we look at a season, it starts with the first practice and goes until the last team gathering (picnic or final game celebration). Coaches have many topics and issues to address with various community and organization people, plus other coaches. Preseason work can be the most important part of the season. For those of you who wear the coach's hat, there is ample time and opportunity to begin coaching from the inside out. Your time and energy spent in this part of the season is an investment. It sets the stage and tone for the entire season.

Traditional time spent is 80 percent on physical skills and 20 percent on mental knowledge. We need to reverse the numbers as much as possible to focus on the mental aspects of the players. Obviously physical abilities are important but we must strongly address the critically powerful areas of game-situation knowledge and motivation. The trick is to combine physical skill drills with our words of positive reinforcement and encouragement. This gets the door open to the inside. While players are turning physical skills into muscle memory, they are freeing their minds to focus on improvement and internal awareness of how their bodies and minds are performing.

Preseason

This is the time to meet with your coaches and determine practice frequency, number of exhibition/pickup games, tournament participation, etc. It is now that you conduct your goal setting plans and discuss any other issues needing clarification. In Chapter 15 dealing with teaching mechanics, we suggested that you establish a calendar notebook. In your early coaches meeting, log in your coaching goals and season plans.

Philosophy

Our coaching philosophy should not be a secret to our players. Early in the practice season—and throughout the entire season—we should communicate our philosophies of the game to the team. General discussions of philosophy include the topics of hard work, emphasizing academic importance, attitude, and goals. You should discuss the fact that each player must earn a spot on the team and nothing is free. Other topics could include the philosophy of:

▲ Hitting
▲ Kicking
▲ Base running
▲ Catching
▲ Conservative offense
▲ Solid defense
▲ Many players turning into one team
▲ Running a route
▲ Quarterbacking

▲ Mental focus

▲ Accepting bad calls

These are just a few. You can see we're not talking about a physical skill. We are addressing how a player should mentally approach a game situation. For example, the philosophy of batting encourages a player to confidently stride up to the plate looking for a ball to hit. The batter should be thinking "swing" on every pitch until the last possible second when the batter determines the ball is unhittable and checks the swing. The philosophy of batting is an awareness of pulling a ball on the inside of the plate, hitting more up the middle on a middle pitch and stepping into an outside pitch and sending it to the opposite direction. The batter must believe he or she owns that plate with the confidence in their ability to hit any ball in any situation. You can see how discussing philosophies of game factors turns the focus to the inside. As you get creative you can incorporate your own "philosophy of..." lessons. These are great topics to discuss during practice breaks taken between physical skill drills as well as other times when you and the team are all together in a discussion setting.

Evaluation

This is simple record keeping. It's a good habit to have because good records help avoid and/or answer complaints. Records on a player's skill development let you provide constructive improvement suggestions of individual mechanics or form (and not the player). It's a good idea to take attendance at practices and make notes during practices. List the players' names and make room for miscellaneous notes and observations. Even if you never use your notes, the act of taking notes sends a message to the team. It says you are constantly monitoring and evaluating their performance, attitude, and behavior. Beware, they'll be curious to know what you are writing, but it's probably not a good idea to let them read your notes. It could be another golden opportunity to talk one-on-one with a player about his or her performance.

Preparation

In the early season coach's meeting, you should develop a written game plan for the practice season. Have a progressive building-block format of practices and skills. Detail the learning points well before the game season begins. There's nothing worse than having all the team's coaches stand in a group before a practice session looking at each other asking, "What are we going to do tonight?" and no one having an answer. Also early in the season is the time to check all gear and repair and replace as needed. And you must address the area of uniforms in questions such as: Do we use last year's? Are they in good shape? Do they need repair? Should you get new pieces? Then communicate the uniform status to players and parents. Last but not least is the area of money. The beginning of the season is the time to budget for all the team's expenses. This avoids surprises and confusion.

Early in the practice season is also the time to discuss the importance of attitude and effort. Tell your young players that their practice starts on day one. Explain what tryouts are and that tryouts go on all season long. Kids need to understand this philosophy early so they can practice and play accordingly.

The next chapter in this section deals with your coaching responsibilities and improvements during the middle of the season.

Chapter Highlights
to Improve Your Game Plan

▲ The sporting season starts with the first practice and ends with the final team gathering/celebration.

▲ Early communication between all coaches is critical for smooth practices and team development.

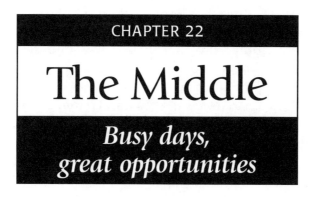

CHAPTER 22

The Middle

Busy days,
great opportunities

Consider the entire season as a voyage on a luxury ocean passenger ship. Once you get out of sight of the starting shore, it's important to know your bearings. As the captain, you need the support of the whole crew to reach your destination. Mid-season offers a great opportunity to determine and discuss where your team has been, where you are today, and the direction your team is heading. It's critical to involve your players in this mid-season analysis and adjustment period. Even if most things are going well, this is a golden opportunity to review and reinforce the positive aspects of the team's development and performance. Celebrate the positives and the successes and identify any areas of needed improvement.

Evaluation

Evaluating individual players and team growth is an ongoing activity. In your calendar notebook you should often jot down your post-practice and post-game notes and thoughts. This is different from maintaining team and player statistics. These notes are your observations of who did what, who needs work, what went well or badly and other observations about the "inside" parts of the game. Bring out those individual goals written down during your one-on-one preseason conversations. Have follow-up discussions with each player to highlight positive areas and encourage continued work on the areas of potential growth. You also can evaluate the recorded team short- and long-term goals set earlier and determine how well the team is doing.

Does this take time? Yes, it does require an investment of time. But for the individual players, there is tremendous benefit in knowing how they're doing. You can help them with mid-season updates and guide them in directions of improvement. Goal setting is a waste of time if you don't periodically meet with the individual player and the team to review the goals and remind everyone where they are in their journey through the season. Mike Krzyzewski writes about goals and adjustments:

> Playing hard together, being the best defensive team, and players building strong bonds with one another, are shared goals that involve working together as a group over the entire year. If a team consistently concentrates on goals like that, major achievements happen.
>
> I think it's also important to remember that if circumstances change during the year, goals might have to change as well. In addition, progress has to be monitored on a regular basis and good work has to be rewarded and encouraged. (Krzyzewski, p. 61)

Adjustments

The middle of your season is a good time to help facilitate physical and mental adjustments to improve overall team performance. Physical adjustments are relatively easy once the skill defect is identified. You can incorporate specific corrections to lessen individual flaws. Mental adjustments are more difficult and force us to deal with all those factors on the inside. We have to focus our efforts on a player's or team's motivation, desire, unity, drive, etc., depending on the problem. You may need to reestablish new goals, either up or down, depending on the team development.

The growth opportunities should be communicated and accepted in a positive way. You play a big role in helping make all team and individual changes. It is a good idea to involve the players in the overall decision-making process. When the players are part of the original and adjusted goals and the decisions made, they'll work harder to attain those goals.

Player Assignments

Here's a scenario on different kinds of coaches that was briefly mentioned in Chapter 6. Imagine your team is not "coming to play" and they don't seem motivated with their "game faces" on. They appear to be bored with you and the whole sporting situation. You determine the team needs a shot in the arm. Here is a strategy worth trying.

If your team has no team captains or co-captains, you might consider transferring some or even a lot of control of the team to the players and a few player leaders. This must be done after a lot of open communication with the entire team. The individuals and team need to provide good constructive criticism of how they see the situation (you could be amazed at what you hear). After the team realizes its lack of a positive attitude or performance or both, they need to take responsibility for where the team has been and its future. If this transfer is successful you will see an immediate turnaround in the team's enthusiasm, pregame attitude, warm-up drills, and game performance. If you and your coaches decide the team needs this kind of adjustment and pursue this approach, you should select the team captain(s) based on their knowledge of the game and acceptance from the rest of the team. If you carefully select the right player, you should check with that player first to ensure he or she wants the responsibility. By transferring overall control and responsibility to the team, you are sending a fantastic message to the team that they are inheriting total control of their own destiny. Make sure the team wants this control. The transfer must occur in a team discussion. And once you embark down this road of handing the reins to the team and their player captains, your role is diminished and you'll often find yourself seeing the team running itself.

Even if you do not assign a player captain, you can still accomplish a successful transfer of team control. Depending on your team makeup and age, the team may assume control of themselves as you methodically give it to them. This transfer can be a gradual thing and if handled properly by you, it creates a sense of responsibility and motivation in every player.

Competitive Level

We have all seen our team play to the level of the competition. We have seen the team play "down" and badly against lesser opponents, and "up" and capably when facing a superior opponent. Our question has always been how to avoid playing down to the lower competitive levels. You'll recognize that this book has addressed how to avoid these variations in performance by practicing strong mental focus and playing "up" to your own team's potential, regardless of the caliber of the opponent. We all want the team to arrive at the field, diamond, or court ready to perform to their best level.

When you become successful in transferring responsibility for the overall individual and team performance to the players, you'll see tremendous results. As part of this transfer, you can make your athletes believe that they hold the key to their own success. They alone can determine how they play and perform. Get your young athletes to believe that the only team that can defeat them is the very team they represent. Your team beats itself. There will always be a superior team you play and lose to, regardless of your own level of performance. But as a general rule, your team should understand and believe they usually control whether they win or lose a game. This becomes a powerful belief attitude within your team players and if you become successful in developing this belief, you will have accomplished much.

Chapter Highlights
to Improve Your Game Plan

▲ Be prepared to make physical and mental adjustments to improve overall team performance.

▲ Get the team to believe that (other things being equal) the only team that can defeat them is themselves.

CHAPTER 23

The Finale

The season's over but not the growth

The season's over. No, how can that be? We just had our first practice "the other day." Things are going so well, it can't be over. Well, as reality sets in, we all must accept the fact that individual seasons must end. Look at it this way. The sadness you're feeling is because the season brought you (and your young athletes) so much joy. If you practice the principles found in this book, you will naturally experience some sadness because a positive thing in your life is temporarily ending. If your heart isn't a little sad, you need to work harder at finding joy through your involvement with young kids.

But don't let your heart be too heavy. Next season isn't far away. For now, you should focus on making the end of this season memorable for everyone. This is not the time to focus on negatives about any individual or the team. Recap the successes. It's a good time to restate the original team goals and how well those goals were achieved. The season finale sets the stage for the future and leaves a lasting impression on the players and parents. At the end of the season, the actual win/loss record doesn't matter. Individual wins and losses become irrelevant with time. What does matter is the development and growth of the kids. It's our job to prepare them for the next seasons. Be philosophical and focus on the big picture.

Building Blocks

Analogy: In every school, in math, science, and English classes, every year is a building block on top of the previous year. Similarly, every season is a building block in the overall participation and personal growth of a young athlete. We coaches must focus on long-term growth and goal accomplishment to help each player develop the proper attitude and perspective toward the game. Kids don't think long-term so we have to do it for them. Another aspect of the end of a season involves conducting a closing meeting with all coaches for the team. This is necessary to recap and review the entire season in preparation for the next year. It's best to conduct this season review while our minds are fresh and before we move on to other activities.

The Next Season

It is a good idea to note all successes and shortcomings from the season just finished. Then the plan for the next season can be improved upon. Start preparing for next season right away as a coach and with the players. As the season ends tell the team to continue practicing on their own. The off-season is a great time to work on physical improvement for the next season. Again, if you parents have made your own "home practices" fun and exciting, your children will want to play with you. Enjoy these no-pressure times of play to be together. And it's never too early to think about gear and equipment for next year. Their bodies grow rapidly. Off-season birthday gifts will need time to get broken in and accustomed to.

The Season after Next

During your last team gathering, discuss the long-term view of youth sports and relate it to the bigger picture. Emphasize individual physical and mental growth. You should address the importance of academics and remind the players that just as in sports, persistence and hard work lead to success. Youth sports are learning opportunities for a variety of other activities and human relationships.

The Seasons of Life

We all go through many seasons of our lives. Time goes by too quickly for those of us enjoying life. And good coaches and parents find no greater happiness than working with kids and helping them grow. By planting a little of our own wisdom and personality into our kids, we nurture a few seeds of our own immortality. Part of us lives on in our kids. Before we know it (and certainly before they know it), our kids will be out of high school and creating new lives of their own. Mike Krzyzewski presents a philosophy of life:

> Every season is a journey. Every journey is a lifetime. Nobody can predict what's going to happen along the way. Some bad things may occur, some great things may come to pass. But whatever happens, like life, the journey should be enjoyed. We ought to soak up the moisture that falls daily—and not allow ourselves to get bogged down in our original plan without adjusting to whatever occurs along our path. That way, we look forward to success on a year-to-year basis. (Krzyzewski, p. 62)

Youth sports are a vehicle for individual growth, advancement, and maturity. The players acquire many long-term memories and lessons to carry with them. As kids grow up and eventually leave youth sports, we want them to look back on their participation in a positive light. Throughout their lives they will practice many of the values promoted in this book because you have instilled them.

Chapter Highlights
to Improve Your Game Plan

▲ Every season should be viewed as a building block in preparation for the next season.

The Future

Notes and Thoughts

CHAPTER 24

Your Program

Successful sports in your community

What will the future of youth sports bring us? Pressures will continue to increase and there will be more and more distractions in the years ahead. We will see our roles and responsibilities expand beyond today's level. And the time we spend helping young athletes will be even more important and critical to the growth of individual players. This chapter brings the future to our attention by looking at what we can all expect as more and more young athletes sign up to participate. Every community, every school, and every organization can vary in their approach and goals. But all will see continued change in the years and decades ahead.

School

A primary trend seen in schools is a stronger focus on participation and a diminished emphasis on winning and scores. In our present-day litigious society, there is growing political correctness in our schools in general. Schools are becoming viewed as gigantic day-care centers where more and more kids of all abilities get involved in sports. Our roles become more important as we compete but we'll have to match overall "fair" participation with the desire to win (remember that winning a game is not as important as striving to win). In many schools there are fewer and fewer sporting dollars for more and more kids, gear, and facilities. Coaches will become increasingly involved in the behind-the-scenes administration and politics of youth sports. This nonteam-related involvement may not be what we want to do but it is a necessary growing requirement in the future of youth sports.

Community

Many communities and cities organize entire groups of teams for various sports. For example, a hundred fifth-graders get split into seven or eight soccer teams with volunteer coaches (usually parents). As adults you have a great opportunity to improve the program, as we'll cover in the next chapter. Community recreation leagues focus on participation for all kinds of kids. We will see every sort of kid with every different ability on our teams. In this type of community-based program, all kids get a chance. Whenever and wherever possible, we should attempt to make changes to allow for more youth involvement and excitement in organized games. If you use your imagination, you could come up with many ideas for your particular sport that could spice up the games and make them much more fun for everyone. Author Jay Coakley agrees that changing a few rules would improve youth sports. He writes:

> Since children have fun by emphasizing action, involvement, close scores, and friendships in the games they create for themselves, it makes sense that organized programs should be restructured to emphasize these things. If this were done, children would have more fun and the programs would do a better job of meeting their interests. (Coakley, p. 126)

Organization

Throughout the country there are many organizations that sponsor a youth sports league or team. Most of these are autonomous groups with their own governing boards, rules and regulations, etc. Here is a sampling: American Youth Football, Babe Ruth Baseball, Little League Baseball, American Youth Soccer Organization, American Junior Golf Association, Christian Sports International, Hap Dumont, Pop Warner Football, Pony Baseball, Sporting

Chance Youth Basketball, T-Ball USA, Tennis Industry Association, Young America Bowling Alliance, YMCA, American Running and Fitness Association, Boys and Girls Clubs of America, VFW, and many others.

Often teams are involved in competition with similar teams from other cities or areas. These are excellent avenues for kids to play a lot and grow in the sport. The teams found in these organizations often conduct tryouts for individual players to make the team. There are usually higher levels of performance, ability, and competition in these types of organized teams. The trend for the future will include more adult control, more adult involvement, and a continued strong focus on individual and team winning. Our job of working from the inside out will become even more critical and serve to balance the ever-growing external focus on winning.

Long-Term Partnership

We coaches have to adopt a big picture long-term vision of our involvement with youth teams. We should continually expand our sphere of contacts within the team-sponsoring unit and help plan for our replacement when we move on or out. We should promote the philosophies of coaching from the inside out and recommend coaches of like mind to work with kids. It is also our responsibility to bring in new coaches whenever appropriate and welcome new ideas to improve the total program.

ConFUNdence

We coach kids to do well and they develop confidence while they're having fun. Most of us are not paid money for these efforts. Consequently, the entire experience should be enjoyable for us too. If not, we'll quit, which would be too bad because we have a lot to offer. In the same way kids stay involved with fun and growing confidence, we also stay involved in coaching if we enjoy the responsibility. Year after year, we all get better at what we're doing. We learn from our successes and failures (just like we teach our players to do). We gain confidence every year. You might say we're no different from the players we coach in the area of fun and confidence, i.e. conFUNdence. These two things go together.

We hold the future in our hands. Regardless of the sport, coaches all have a more important role than most realize. As a group, we have a huge influence in the long-term success or failure of our sporting programs.

Chapter Highlights
to Improve Your Game Plan

▲ Youth sports in the future will see many philosophical and organizational changes.

▲ The trend of more organization by adults and parental involvement will continue to grow.

Coach Unity

Get on the same page

Put yourself into the shoes of a young player just beginning a sport. Pretend that in the first year you have a few coaches with their own terminology and techniques. They have certain ways they want you to do specific things. Then the next year you have different coaches with different terms and philosophies. Year after year you get new and conflicting instructions. In schools, communities, and organizations all over the country kids are subjected to inconsistent coaching conditions that are easily avoidable. We coaches must first be aware of how we as a group present our sport and then ensure we are doing it for the maximum betterment of all kids involved.

Human Involvement

In any program there are many other people involved besides the coach. Coaches are not alone. There are administrators, other coaches, parents, and other interested parties. It is our job as coach to carry out the goals of the overall youth program. We are the ones executing the game plan of the community organization. It is incumbent upon us to do the best we can within the circle of individuals and objectives placed in front of us.

Program Development

Have you ever noticed (and asked yourself "why") year after year the program loses players? We have discussed various reasons dealing with motivation and drive. Another major explanation involves a lack of continuity in major aspects of the sporting program. Not all coaches within the same sport are on the same page when it comes to instruction formats, basic skills, techniques, terms, and philosophies.

We coaches are in an excellent position to help develop program continuity, by streamlining our overall efforts. We must work with program organizers to develop and implement standards of coaching. Here's a typical situation. Early in every season we start with a group of kids at different levels of fundamental ability and knowledge. Much of the time we're teaching basics that should have been taught correctly in earlier years. We can promote year after year consistency by developing age appropriate basic building block skills that are taught by every coach for each age in the same way. This will help all players as they change teams and coaches in subsequent years. Players will know more, their basic techniques will be consistent, they will perform better and enjoy the game more. This makes it easier for us coaches to advance into higher mental and physical levels of the game.

Coach Communications

Thorough and frequent communications between all coaches are critical to developing solid coaching unity. We just presented a sample situation pertaining to a group of coaches who all have teams of similar age. They must communicate, develop, and implement a unified approach. But how about a program with progressive levels of teams at different ages? For example, there are many kids involved in baseball or basketball from age 8 to 18. Within the various team opportunities over this 10-year span, a player will see many coaches as he or she progresses through different organizations.

To promote a unified consistent approach, coaches of all ages and groups should interact and create a single best format for program advancement. You as a coach need to talk with coaches above your level and below your level. You'll be amazed at their expectations, assumptions, and requirements. Advanced coaches will have specific needs and suggestions for overall improvement. Coaches beneath your team level probably won't be aware of your needs and experiences. You've been in their shoes and could offer them a lot of help.

A good method to maintain and enhance total coach/program unity is to have individual representatives (coaches and others) form a sports board that meets to conduct all aspects of a unified body. This group should communicate all agreed-upon techniques and terminologies. They will create a singular strategy as it pertains to the entire big picture program. As a result, they could publish a simple handbook spelling out all goals and objectives, plus how the board and coaches will carry out those objectives. The board guidebook will include all age appropriate instruction techniques and all other critical information. Parents will see this booklet and be on the same page with the rest of the total program.

Assistant Coach Roles

All coaches are important and have critical roles in the growth and advancement of young athletes. Different kids click or bond with different coaches. For the purposes of this book there has been no distinction made between head coaches and assistant coaches. Obviously the head coach has various expanded roles (often in the administrative and coordination areas) above and beyond assistants. Head coaches end up doing most of the parent communication work and most team discipline. But good assistants who practice the philosophies prescribed in this book are a valuable asset to the head coach and the team. The assistant is on an equal level with the head coach when it comes to successful coaching from the inside out.

Players see assistant coaches as authority figures similar to the head coach. The role of an assistant coach is to help present a unified message to all players of what is expected of the team. The assistant acts like a clone of the head coach and must be identical to the head coach in training and instruction. Assistants are often called upon to make decisions and step in if the head coach is temporarily absent.

Assistant coaches have a variety of responsibilities. They must support and practice the head coach's techniques. This includes the overall mental and philosophical approach. If there is ever a case where the assistant disagrees with the head coach, it is never appropriate to do so in view of the team. Any differences or questions must be conducted and resolved in private. Assistants have to help the entire team by communicating successes and failures to the other coaches. Every coach has strengths and areas of expertise to draw from and all coaches can benefit from each other's wisdom. Also, assistants can help the head coaches in some of the administrative responsibilities. They are valuable in helping run practices and games. Just as it takes a team effort by the players to perform well and achieve team goals, it takes a unified coaching team effort to achieve specific goals.

Coaching the Game Versus Coaching Individual Players

There are two different approaches to how we look at a game. We can focus all our energies on the game strategies, game situations, and game outcomes. The obvious pitfalls include a misdirected focus on winning (instead of striving to win) and the score becomes more important than individual and team development for the long haul.

The other approach involves coaching individual players. This method de-emphasizes winning. It focuses instead on all the things discussed in this book. But there is a potential pitfall if we ignore all scores and wins/losses (your team won't allow you to completely ignore winning). The pitfall would be to eliminate any thought of winning or the associated risks of losing. Both can be great learning situations.

Our job is to walk the fine line between both approaches and use the positives of both with our team. As we have shown, our emphasis of striving to win (instead of winning at all costs) mixed with the long-term development of the individual player will produce the best results.

186

So to recap, it should be apparent to you by now that coaching has evolved from just showing up with a ball to a position of incredible responsibility and human reward. Things have changed since the early days of coaching kids and we must all deal with many more factors. Today's world is vastly different from when we were kids. We have looked at the psychology of players and the team, and the internal areas of discipline, anger, and success. We've looked at all the roles we play in young lives and how we teach values. We've discussed the roles of all adults in this complicated picture and how to view various parts of the entire season. Let's now go deep inside, not the individual player or the team, but ourselves.

Chapter Highlights
to Improve Your Game Plan

▲ Coaches should interact with other coaches above and below their own levels to exchange critical information for the growth of the overall program.

▲ Coaches and other interested adults should join or form a governing board to oversee smooth program operation.

▲ A guidebook of goals and philosophies is a good idea to communicate to all parents and new coaches.

CHAPTER 26

Perspective

With proper perspective, everybody wins!

This is the most important chapter in the whole book. The discussion of perspective has been saved until last to sum up our total objective outlook on the complete topic of youth sports. Throughout your entire season, every season, this is the chapter you must refer to over and over again. The wrong perspective will ensure that we and our kids have negative memories. The wrong perspective will lead to attitudes and beliefs contrary to the positive approach promoted in all the previous chapters. The wrong perspective will keep us on a path of just going through the motions of guiding young people without reaping any of the potentially tremendous rewards.

The correct perspective will enable us to relish every moment during and after the season. We will look at our experience with an inner peace and satisfaction found only in coaches and parents with a positive true perspective. We have covered a lot of ground. You might say each chapter and philosophy is a spoke in the wheel of a bike. This chapter is the hub that holds it all together. Many ideas, thoughts, and suggestions have been presented. There are various avenues for us all to reach our common goals if we focus on guiding young athletes from the inside out within a framework of proper perspective.

Coaches, Players, Parents

Let's get introspective and ask ourselves a few questions from the standpoint of a coach, a player, and lastly, a parent. First as a coach. We all must ask ourselves, "What do we want to gain from our coaching experience?" "Where do we offer our best contributions?" "How do I want to be remembered by my players?"

Players need the proper perspective on sports also. You must help them in this area. They need to ask themselves the following simple questions: "Why am I here?" "What if I make a mistake or miss a shot?" "Will my family still love me?" "Will I have the things that are important to me? My home, my health, etc?" The answers to most of these questions are obvious. Players must know that if they have a bad inning or quarter or match or game, it's not the end of the world.

And finally, every parent must ask: "Do I want my child to remember my involvement in this sport as an embarrassing loudmouth arguing with coaches, umpires, and other parents? Or as a quiet, loving, consoling, supportive parent always at the games whenever possible and always seeming to know what my child is thinking and feeling?"

Reality Check

Every artist from time to time steps back from the masterpiece and analyzes it from a distance. We coaches and parents periodically need to do likewise. Face it, sometimes we're not the best we can be or should be. We all slip once in a while even when we are trying to practice the principles of molding young athletes from the inside out. We all are prone to do a goofy thing, say a wrong thing, or act out some other "second-guessable" behavior. We are a continuing work in progress. We all have a goal to attain. We all are trying to reach our own definition of success by striving to achieve. But alas, we never quite make it and this is good. We have high standards for ourselves. Sound familiar? It should, because we encourage our young athletes to place the same high standards on themselves. It's our style. We cannot avoid it. It's how we approach any aspect of our lives, including striving to improve, striving for goals, and striving to do our best. When you feel inadequate or like you've let down the principles of guiding kids from the inside out, do not give up or get discouraged. Keep working on it. You can't quit (what would you tell your young athlete?). Keep identifying areas of needed improvement in yourself (just like the team) and work to improve.

Fun

Fun equates to and results in the best performance. This is true in every endeavor, not just youth sports. Take your job, for example. If you approach your job with a positive attitude incorporating many of the philosophies prescribed in this book, you will perform better. On the opposite side of the coin, if you approach your job and co-workers with negativity and disdain, you'll be miserable. If money was not an object, how long would you stay involved and participate? If you stay in these negative situations, you will not perform to the best of your ability. It's simple. An attitude of fun and personal enjoyment will result in the highest performance.

Now, we'll end with a few final questions and thoughts for you to consider. Time has an incredible way of helping us all put things in their proper perspective. Here are some time thoughts.

We need to stop and examine our "life as a coach or a parent." We'll close by asking ourselves the following questions and begin thinking about some solid deeper answers. Then we need to behave in a way to match our truthful answers to these questions. Here's a simple yet thought-provoking analogy. Project yourself out 100 years and foresee what wording you want on your gravestone (great father/mother, wonderful husband/wife, Godly person). The secret to life is to then work toward living up to those words. On a lesser scale, we can view our role in a similar way.

A few final questions to ask yourself:

▲ "In 10 years will I have enjoyed my time investment with young people?"

▲ "Will I be able to say I made a difference in the life of a young person?"

▲ "When a young athlete I coached has grown into a parent or a coach on their own, will they remember me positively?"

▲ "Will my kids have pleasant memories of me?"

▲ "Will they adopt some of the philosophies I used and practice some of the values they learned when they were with me?"

▲ "Will I believe I did something good and have positive thoughts about my involvement?"

▲ "In 50 years, as on older person sitting in my rocking chair, will I have fond memories of my times with youth sports programs and young adult athletes?"

▲ "Will I have had an effect on the future of our world?"

▲ "Was being a coach good for my players?"

▲ "Was I a good parent of a young athlete?"

▲ "Did I do well?"

Your single answer will be, "Yes, I think I did. In a small way, in my small little world, I did my best. And just like the belief I instilled into all my kids, when the game is over, I can walk off the field with my head held high. I did my best. That's all I ever asked of my kids and that's all I can ask of myself."

Pictures In Your Mind

Look back to those early precious days
Of babies and toddlers
They were so dependent on us parents
We felt unprepared, but accepted the tasks

The early years
Walking, running, falling, laughing, crying
They needed us more every day
To help them, to talk with them, to hold them

Then school and friends and teachers
Dogs and cats and natural wonders
Can you see them running in your backyard,
    laughing, playing
Life and time stood still, it was just like yesterday

Then came their first sporting activity
They looked so small
Can you still picture the big uniforms they wore
Their gear seemed so big

Season after season passed
More friends, more independence
What incredible gifts we've been blessed with
But we still feel somewhat inadequate for the task
    of raising a child

More games, trying different sports, more friends
And our roles remain the same
To support them, to play with them
To love them

Seems like time is passing quicker than before
Everybody's so busy growing up

It's wonderful but there's so much to do
They grow so quickly before our very eyes

Can you see them as young teenagers
Almost young adults
How can this be
The picture in your mind is still of the young
   toddler, depending on you

Then there are freshman dances
Junior proms
Homecoming events
And in a flash, high school graduations, already

Soon they're gone
Away from our home
Out on their own
Starting a new life

Picture them in the delivery room becoming new
   parents
If they could only know the things you know
They'd slow down
They'd work less
They'd play catch more often
They'd have more patience
They'd let the grass grow a little longer
They'd wait to dust the furniture one more day
They'd love more
They'd play more
They will create their own pictures from their own
   memories

The photo albums in our minds are getting full
Every picture is a gift
Every picture is a blessing from God, if
We choose to make them so

—*Darrell Erickson*

194

BIBLIOGRAPHY

Bassett, Lucinda. *From Panic to Power: Proven Techniques to Calm Your Anxieties, Conquer Your Fears and Put You in Control of Your Life.* New York: HarperCollins, 1995.

Bromfield, Richard, Ph.D. *Handle With Care: Understanding Children and Teachers.* New York: Teachers College Press, 2000.

Brown, Les. *It's Not Over Until You Win!: How to Become the Person You Always Wanted to Be—No Matter What the Obstacle.* New York: Simon and Schuster, 1997.

Burt, Sandra, and Linda Perlis. *Parents as Mentors: A New Perspective on Parenting That Can Change Your Child's Life.* Rocklin, CA: Prima, 1999.

Coakley, Jay J. *Sport in Society: Issues And Controversies.* St. Louis, Missouri: Mosby-Year Book, 1994.

Dlugokinski, Eric, Ph.D., and Sandra Allen, Ph.D. *Empowering Children to Cope with Difficulty and Build Muscles for Mental Health.* Washington, DC: Taylor & Francis, 1997.

Kauss, David, Ph.D. *Mastering Your Inner Game: A Self-Guided Approach to Finding Your Unique Sports Performance Keys.* Champaign, IL: Human Kinetics, 2001.

Krzyzewski, Mike. *Leading With the Heart.* New York: Warner Books, 2000.

Lynch, Jerry, Ph.D., and Chungliang Al Huang. *Working Out, Working Within: The Tao of Inner Fitness Through Sports and Fitness.* New York: Penguin Putnam, 1998.

Mack, Gary. *Mind Gym: An Athlete's Guide to Inner Excellence.* New York: Contemporary, 2001.

Margenau, Eric, Ph.D. *Sports Without Pressure: A Guide for Parents and Coaches of Young Athletes.* New York: Gardner Press, 1990.

Meltz, Barbara. *Put Yourself in Their Shoes: Understanding How Your Children See the World.* New York: Dell, 1999.

Murphy, Shane, Ph.D. *The Achievement Zone: 8 Skills for Winning All the Time from the Playing Field to the Boardroom.* New York: G.P. Putnam's Sons, 1996.

National Alliance for Youth Sports, Member's Handbook, West Palm Beach, Florida.

Perry, Dr. Mitchell, and Steve Jamison. *In the Zone: Achieving Optimal Performance in Business—As in Sports.* New York: Contemporary, 1997.

Pickhardt, Carl, Ph.D. *Keys to Developing Your Child's Self-Esteem.* Hauppauge, NY: Barron's, 2000.

Potter, Dr. Beverly. *From Conflict to Cooperation: How to Mediate a Dispute.* Berkeley, CA: Ronin, 1996.

Powell, Dr. Trevor. *Stress Free Living.* New York: DK Publishing, 2000.

Rimm, Dr. Sylvia. *Dr. Sylvia Rimm's Smart Parenting: How to Raise a Happy, Achieving Child.* New York: Crown, 1996.

Sugarman, Karlene, M.A. *Winning the Mental Way: A Practical Guide to Team Building and Mental Training.* Burlingame, CA: Step Up Publishing, 1998.

Youngs, Bettie B., Ph.D., Ed.D. *Stress and Your Child: Helping Kids Cope with the Strains and Pressures of Life.* New York: Ballantine Books, 1995.

INDEX

197

Give the Gift of
Molding Young Athletes
to Your Friends and Colleagues

CHECK YOUR LEADING BOOKSTORE OR ORDER HERE

❑ **YES**, I want _____ copies of *Molding Young Athletes* at $14.95 each, plus $4.95 shipping per book (Wisconsin residents please add 82¢ sales tax per book). Canadian orders must be accompanied by a postal money order in U.S. funds. Allow 15 days for delivery.

❑ **YES**, I am interested in having Darrell Erickson speak or give a seminar to my company, association, school, or organization. Please send information.

My check or money order for $_____ is enclosed.

Please charge my: ❑ Visa   ❑ MasterCard
                           ❑ Discover   ❑ American Express

Name _____

Organization _____

Address _____

City/State/Zip _____

Phone_____   E-mail _____

Card # _____

Exp. Date_____ Signature _____

Please make your check payable and return to:
Purington Press
POB 170 • Oregon, WI 53575-0170
Call your credit card order to: 608-873-8723
Fax: 608-873-8723   **www.puringtonpress.com**

Author's Note: Thank you for helping kids to enjoy their games.